THINK.
ADAPT.
LEAD.

CRITICAL THINKING AND ADAPTIVE LEADERSHIP IN AN EVER-CHANGING WORLD

Allan Matthew Lee

Copyright © Allan Matthew Lee 2025
All Rights Reserved.

ISBN 979-8-89744-594-3

This book has been published with all efforts taken to make the material error-free after the consent of the author. However, the author and the publisher do not assume and hereby disclaim any liability to any party for any loss, damage, or disruption caused by errors or omissions, whether such errors or omissions result from negligence, accident, or any other cause.

While every effort has been made to avoid any mistake or omission, this publication is being sold on the condition and understanding that neither the author nor the publishers or printers would be liable in any manner to any person by reason of any mistake or omission in this publication or for any action taken or omitted to be taken or advice rendered or accepted on the basis of this work. For any defect in printing or binding the publishers will be liable only to replace the defective copy by another copy of this work then available.

To my best friend and wife Angelene Marie, my daughter Audrey-Ann and my son Adrian Mark, who have always been the pillars of support in everything I do.

TABLE OF CONTENTS

INTRODUCTION

In an era of rapid technological advancements, geopolitical shifts, and unprecedented global challenges, the ability to think critically and lead adaptively has never been more crucial. The world is accelerating, and leaders across industries must navigate complexity, uncertainty, and ambiguity with agility and foresight. Critical thinking and adaptive leadership are not just skills — they are essential mindsets that enable individuals and organizations to thrive in a dynamic and unpredictable environment.

Critical thinking is the foundation of effective decision-making and problem-solving. It involves analyzing information objectively, evaluating evidence, and considering multiple perspectives before arriving at a well-reasoned conclusion. In a world inundated with data, misinformation, and competing narratives, critical thinking acts as a compass, guiding individuals to discern truth from noise.

Leaders who cultivate critical thinking skills are better equipped to identify root causes instead of addressing symptoms, critical thinkers delve deeper to uncover the underlying issues driving challenges. They can anticipate consequences better and make informed decisions that minimize risks and maximize opportunities by evaluating potential outcomes. Critical thinking fosters innovation by encouraging questioning assumptions and exploring unconventional solutions, paving the way for creativity and innovation. In times of crisis, thinking clearly and logically helps leaders remain calm and focused, inspiring confidence in their teams. However, critical thinking alone is not enough. Leaders must embrace adaptability in a world where change is the only constant.

Adaptive leadership is the ability to respond effectively to changing circumstances, learn from experience, and adjust strategies in real time. Unlike traditional leadership models that rely on rigid hierarchies and fixed plans, adaptive leadership is fluid, collaborative, and responsive. It recognizes that solutions to complex problems often emerge through experimentation, iteration, and collective effort.

"THINK. ADAPT. LEAD." is a concept that involves being flexible and responsive to change and using that flexibility to drive success. To achieve this, we must demonstrate adaptive thinking skills and encourage a growth mindset, empowering ourselves and our teams to act independently and make choices. In doing this, we must establish an adaptive operating rhythm by allowing regular check-ins and adjustments. Through this concept, we train ourselves to make the best decision possible given what we know at the present time. Situational leadership refers to the core concept of constantly assessing a situation, adjusting your leadership style accordingly, and acting based on the needs of your team members or the circumstances at hand; essentially, being flexible and responsive to different situations to effectively lead others.

Critical thinking and adaptive leadership are deeply interconnected. Critical thinking provides the analytical rigor needed to understand complex problems, while adaptive leadership offers the flexibility to respond effectively. Together, they enable leaders to navigate uncertainty by combining logical analysis with a willingness to experiment, leaders can chart a course through uncharted territory. This will drive sustainable change as critical thinking ensures that decisions are well-informed, while adaptability allows for course corrections as new information emerges. Leaders who demonstrate both critical thinking and adaptability earn the trust of their teams, fostering a culture of collaboration and shared purpose.

We then learn to incorporate situational leadership into the concept: analyze the situation and understand the maturity level of your team members in terms of their ability and willingness to take on a task. Based on our analysis, we adjust our leadership style to fit the situation, whether it means providing more direction (telling), coaching and explaining (selling), collaborating (participating), or delegating responsibility based on the team's competency. Once we have identified the appropriate leadership style, we need to actively guide and support our team in achieving the desired outcome.

Incorporating situational leadership into a book about critical and adaptive thinking creates a powerful synergy, as both emphasize flexibility and responsiveness to complex, ever-changing environments. The post-COVID-19 world, marked by uncertainty, technological shifts, and social challenges, demands these skills more than ever. Situational leadership, which adapts leadership styles to the needs of individuals and situations, aligns seamlessly with critical and adaptive thinking, enabling leaders to navigate multifaceted challenges effectively.

Critical thinking allows individuals to analyze complex problems, identify root causes, and develop solutions, while adaptive thinking fosters resilience and the ability to pivot in response to rapid changes. Situational leadership complements these skills by enabling leaders to tailor their approach to the specific context — whether directive, coaching, supportive, or delegative. For example, a directive style may be necessary during a crisis like a new COVID-19 variant, while a collaborative approach might be better suited for long-term recovery planning.

The pandemic accelerated digital transformation, remote work, and global interconnectedness, creating new challenges and opportunities. Critical thinking helps assess the benefits and risks of these changes, while adaptive thinking enables effective integration. Situational leadership supports this transition by guiding employees through unfamiliar technologies or work models. For instance, new remote workers may need a directive or coaching style, while experienced employees thrive with greater autonomy.

Mental health and social resilience have also been tested, requiring leaders to balance empathy with accountability. Situational leadership's emphasis on emotional intelligence helps address these needs, fostering a supportive environment where employees feel valued. Additionally, ethical dilemmas, such as vaccine distribution and privacy concerns, demand critical thinking to evaluate options and adaptive thinking to adjust as societal norms evolve. Situational leaders can navigate these challenges by balancing compliance with collaboration.

Innovation and preparedness are critical in the post-pandemic world. Critical thinking encourages creativity, while adaptive thinking enables experimentation. Situational leadership fosters innovation by tailoring styles to creative teams, such as using a coaching style for brainstorming or a delegative style for empowering experimentation. Similarly, leaders can use a directive style during crises and a supportive style in recovery phases, ensuring resilience against future disruptions.

Social and economic inequalities exacerbated by the pandemic require systemic solutions. Critical thinking helps address these issues, while adaptive thinking promotes inclusive strategies. Situational leadership supports equity by recognizing unique needs — using a supportive style to empower marginalized employees or a coaching style to mentor underrepresented groups.

Critical, adaptive, and situational thinking complement each other in personal, professional, and leadership contexts. Critical thinking provides the foundation for analysis, adaptive thinking enables flexibility, and situational thinking ensures context-specific responses. Together, they enhance decision-making, resilience, and innovation, empowering individuals and leaders to thrive in an uncertain world. By integrating situational leadership with critical and adaptive thinking, leaders can effectively navigate post-pandemic complexities, driving resilience, innovation, and growth in their organizations and communities. These interconnected skills create a robust framework for addressing challenges, fostering inclusivity, and building a more equitable future.

In a world characterized by volatility, uncertainty, complexity, and ambiguity (VUCA), critical thinking and adaptive leadership are indispensable. They empower individuals and organizations to navigate challenges, seize opportunities, and positively impact an ever-changing landscape. By cultivating these skills, leaders can survive and thrive, shaping a resilient, innovative, and inclusive future. As the pace of change accelerates, the ability to think critically and lead adaptively will remain a defining factor in achieving long-term success.

This book aims to equip readers with the essential skills of **critical thinking, adaptive thinking, and situational thinking** to thrive in the post-COVID-19 world. It aims to provide a comprehensive framework for navigating the complexities, uncertainties, and rapid changes that define our current era. By blending theory, practical strategies, and real-world examples, the book will empower individuals, professionals, and leaders to make informed decisions, adapt to challenges, and lead effectively in personal, professional, and organizational contexts.

Readers will understand what critical, adaptive, and situational thinking entails, how they differ, and why they are essential today. They will learn how these skills complement each other and how to apply them in various contexts. The book will provide actionable tools, techniques, and frameworks for developing and applying these thinking skills.

Readers will learn how to analyze complex problems, evaluate information critically, make well-reasoned decisions, and gain the ability to anticipate challenges, identify opportunities, and develop innovative solutions.

The book will teach readers how to embrace change, manage uncertainty, and confidently adapt to new circumstances. They will learn strategies for building personal and professional resilience in disruption.

Leaders will gain insights into how to tailor their leadership style to different situations, teams, and challenges by inspiring and guiding others through uncertainty, fostering collaboration, and driving organizational success.

Readers will develop a growth mindset, enabling them to continuously learn, improve, and thrive in dynamic environments. They will also gain the confidence to tackle challenges, seize opportunities, and achieve their goals.

The book will provide a roadmap for applying these skills to build a more resilient, innovative, and equitable future. Readers will learn how to prepare for and respond to future disruptions, ensuring long-term success and well-being.

The post-COVID-19 world has highlighted the need for individuals and organizations to think critically, adapt quickly, and respond effectively to unprecedented challenges. This book addresses this need by providing a practical, actionable guide to developing the skills to navigate uncertainty, drive innovation, and lead purposefully.

This book will give readers the knowledge, tools, and confidence to survive and thrive in an ever-changing world. They will be equipped to turn challenges into opportunities, lead with resilience, and create a positive impact in their personal lives, workplaces, and communities.

PART 1

FOUNDATIONS OF CRITICAL THINKING

"When your mind is full of assumptions, conclusions, and beliefs, it has no penetration, it just repeats past impressions."

– Sadhguru

Critical thinking is an analytical skill that can unlock the full potential of your mind. Critical thinking has never been more crucial in today's rapidly evolving society, where information is abundant but discerning its validity is becoming increasingly challenging.

Critical thinking is a fundamental skill that allows individuals to analyze, evaluate, and interpret information objectively and rationally. It goes beyond merely accepting information at face value; critical thinkers are equipped to delve deeper, question assumptions, and explore various perspectives before arriving at well-informed conclusions. Critical thinking ability is highly valued across various domains, including education, business, and everyday life.

Chapter 1

CRITICAL THINKING AND THE THINKING PROCESS

1.1 WHAT IS CRITICAL THINKING AND WHY IS IT IMPORTANT

Critical thinking is a disciplined process of actively analyzing, evaluating, and synthesizing information to make reasoned judgments or decisions. It involves questioning assumptions, identifying biases, and applying logical reasoning to solve problems or navigate complex situations. Today, the world is inundated with information, critical thinking is essential for distinguishing fact from fiction, making informed decisions, and addressing challenges effectively. Critical thinking has become indispensable, particularly in the workplace, where complexity, uncertainty, and rapid change are the norm.

CRITICAL THINKING HAS BECOME A REQUIRED PREREQUISITE IN THE MODERN WORKING WORLD.

The digital age has made information more accessible than ever but has also created an overwhelming flood of data, opinions, and misinformation. In the workplace, employees and leaders must sift through vast amounts of information to identify what is relevant, accurate, and useful. Critical thinking enables individuals to evaluate sources, discern credible information from unreliable content, and make decisions based on evidence rather than assumptions or hearsay. For example, a marketing professional analyzing campaign performance data must use critical thinking to separate meaningful metrics from irrelevant noise and draw actionable insights.

Modern workplaces are characterized by complex, multifaceted challenges that rarely have straightforward solutions. Whether addressing supply chain disruptions, developing innovative products, or managing cross-functional teams, critical thinking is essential for breaking down problems into manageable components, analyzing root causes, and developing effective solutions. For instance, a project manager facing delays might use critical thinking to identify bottlenecks, evaluate potential fixes, and implement strategies to get back on track.

The pace of change in today's world — driven by technological advancements, economic shifts, and global events like the COVID-19 pandemic — requires individuals and organizations to be agile and adaptable. Critical thinking empowers employees to assess new situations, anticipate potential challenges, and adjust strategies accordingly. For example, during the pandemic, businesses that relied on critical thinking could pivot quickly to remote work, adopt new technologies, and find innovative ways to serve customers.

Decisions often have far-reaching consequences in the workplace, affecting teams, customers, and the organization. Critical thinking ensures that decisions are well-reasoned, evidence-based, and aligned with organizational goals. It involves weighing pros and cons, considering alternative perspectives, and anticipating potential outcomes. For example, a financial analyst deciding on investment opportunities must use critical thinking to evaluate risks, assess market trends, and make recommendations that align with the company's financial objectives.

Innovation is a key driver of success in today's competitive landscape. Critical thinking encourages individuals to question the status quo, challenge assumptions, and explore new ideas. By analyzing existing processes and identifying areas for improvement, employees can develop creative solutions that drive growth and efficiency. For instance, a software developer might use critical thinking to identify inefficiencies in a system and design a more streamlined solution.

Effective teamwork relies on clear communication and the ability to reconcile diverse perspectives. Critical thinking helps individuals articulate their ideas clearly, support their arguments with evidence, and engage in constructive dialogue. It also enables team members to objectively evaluate each other's contributions and work together to solve problems. For example, during a brainstorming session, critical thinking ensures that ideas are thoroughly evaluated and refined before implementation.

The modern workplace is often characterized by uncertainty, whether it is due to market volatility, technological disruptions, or global crises. Critical thinking equips individuals to navigate ambiguity by analyzing available information, identifying potential risks, and making informed decisions despite incomplete data. For example, a business leader facing an economic downturn might use critical thinking to assess the situation, explore contingency plans, and guide the organization through the crisis.

In an era where ethical considerations are increasingly important, critical thinking helps individuals evaluate the moral implications of their decisions. It involves considering the impact on stakeholders, weighing competing values, and ensuring that actions align with ethical standards. For instance, a company deciding on a new supplier might use critical thinking to assess both cost and quality and the supplier's labor practices and environmental impact.

Critical thinking fosters a mindset of curiosity, reflection, and continuous improvement. By regularly evaluating their thought processes and learning from mistakes, individuals can build resilience and adapt to new challenges. This is particularly important in a world where skills and knowledge quickly become outdated. For example, in a rapidly evolving field like artificial intelligence, professionals must use critical thinking to stay updated on new developments and continuously refine their expertise.

Critical thinking is crucial to career development and success in different industries and positions. For example, in management, where decision-making is associated with the daily functioning of an organization, critical thinking plays a crucial role. With good critical thinking skills, managers can resolve complex problems independently and collaboratively, always striving for innovative solutions. In addition, improved critical thinking skills can establish oneself as an adept member of the organization and enhance the quality of life. In today's dynamic work environment, where situations are often uncertain and ambiguous, critical thinking skills can make a difference between success and failure, both professionally and personally.

Ultimately, critical thinking is a cornerstone of organizational success. It enables employees at all levels to contribute to strategic goals, solve problems effectively, and adapt to changing circumstances. Organizations prioritizing critical thinking are better equipped to innovate, compete, and thrive in a dynamic environment. For example, a company that encourages critical thinking at all levels is likelier to identify emerging opportunities, address challenges proactively, and maintain a competitive edge.

In today's working world, critical thinking is not just a valuable skill but a prerequisite for success. It empowers individuals to navigate complexity, make informed decisions, and adapt to change while fostering innovation, collaboration, and ethical behavior. As the workplace evolves, thinking critically will remain essential for individuals and organizations, ensuring resilience, growth, and long-term success in an increasingly uncertain and interconnected world.

1.2 KEY COMPONENTS OF CRITICAL THINKING

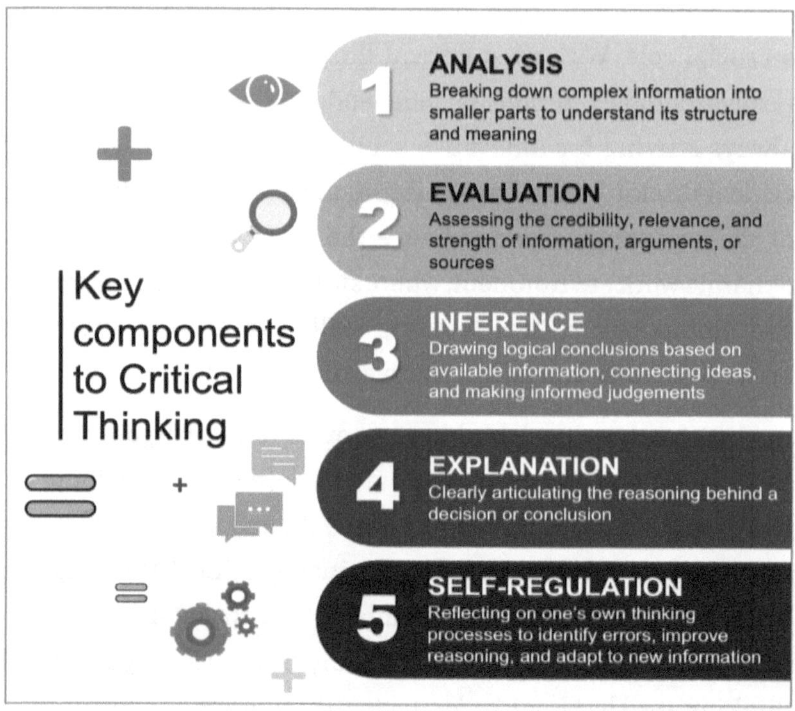

Critical thinking comprises several key components: analysis, evaluation, inference, explanation, and self-regulation.

Analysis involves breaking down complex information into smaller, more manageable parts to understand its structure and meaning better. This process includes carefully examining evidence, identifying patterns or trends, and understanding how different ideas or components relate. For example, when analyzing a problem, one might dissect it into its root causes, contributing factors, and potential impacts to better understand the issue at hand. This foundational step allows individuals to organize information systematically and prepare for deeper evaluation.

Evaluation assesses information, arguments, and sources' credibility, relevance, and strength. This involves questioning the validity of evidence, such as checking whether data is accurate, up-to-date, and from a reliable source. It also requires recognizing biases — both in the information being evaluated and within oneself — and identifying logical fallacies that may weaken an argument. For instance, when evaluating a news article, one might consider the author's expertise, the publication's reputation, and whether the claims are supported by credible evidence. This step ensures that decisions are based on sound and trustworthy information.

Inference is the process of drawing logical conclusions based on the information available. It requires individuals to connect ideas, predict potential outcomes, and make informed judgments. For example, if data shows a consistent increase in sales after a marketing campaign, one might infer that the campaign was effective. Inference often involves using inductive or deductive reasoning to bridge information gaps and arrive at well-supported conclusions. This step is crucial for problem-solving and decision-making, allowing individuals to move from raw data to actionable insights.

Explanation entails clearly articulating the reasoning behind a decision or conclusion. This involves communicating ideas effectively, whether through writing, speaking, or other forms of expression, and justifying one's thought process in a way that is logical and easy to follow. For example, a manager explaining a strategic decision to their team might outline the data analyzed, the alternatives considered, and the rationale for the chosen course of action. Effective explanation clarifies one's thinking and helps others understand and engage with the reasoning process.

Self-regulation involves reflecting on one's thinking processes to identify errors, improve reasoning, and adapt to new information. This includes being open to feedback, acknowledging mistakes, and revising conclusions when necessary. For instance, if new evidence contradicts a previously held belief, a critical thinker will reassess their position rather than cling to outdated views. Self-regulation also involves monitoring cognitive biases and emotional responses to ensure they do not unduly influence judgment. This step is essential for continuous learning and growth, as it fosters a mindset of humility and adaptability.

These components — analysis, evaluation, inference, explanation, and self-regulation — form the core of critical thinking. They enable individuals to approach problems systematically, make well-reasoned decisions, and communicate their ideas effectively. By mastering these skills, individuals can confidently navigate complex situations, adapt to changing circumstances, and contribute to meaningful solutions in both personal and professional contexts.

Using critical thinking effectively involves developing a structured approach to analyzing information, solving problems, and making decisions. Here is a step-by-step guide to applying critical thinking in practical, real-world situations.

To effectively incorporate critical thinking into daily practices, we need to cultivate self-awareness. Firstly, we need to use open-ended questions to explore ideas and challenge assumptions. For example, "Why?", "How?", and "What if?" would be good ways to probe and extract more insights.

STAY CURIOUS

Cultivating a mindset of curiosity and a willingness to learn helps with using critical thinking effectively since they are essential for personal growth, professional success, and adaptability in an ever-changing world. Curiosity drives innovation and creativity by encouraging us to ask questions, explore new ideas, and challenge the status quo, leading to groundbreaking solutions and discoveries. It also fosters adaptability, enabling us to navigate rapid changes in technology, industries, and societal norms, ensuring we remain relevant and resilient in the face of challenges. Curiosity enhances problem-solving skills by promoting deeper exploration and understanding of issues, while building resilience by framing setbacks as opportunities for growth. It expands our knowledge and expertise, which is crucial in today's knowledge-based economy, and improves decision-making by encouraging us to consider diverse perspectives and conduct thorough analyses.

Moreover, curiosity strengthens relationships through empathy and active listening, fostering collaboration and trust. It sets us apart in competitive environments by demonstrating proactive learning and fresh thinking. Curiosity cultivates a growth mindset, empowering us to embrace challenges and view failures as learning opportunities while enriching our lives with purpose and fulfillment through exploration and discovery.

Curiosity fuels continuous personal and professional growth, encourages critical thinking, and equips us to thrive in a dynamic world. It is not just a trait but an indispensable tool for success, happiness, and long-term resilience. Let us embrace curiosity and commit to lifelong learning, which is the foundation of a brighter, more innovative, and adaptable future.

PRACTICE ACTIVE LISTENING

Active listening is a cornerstone of critical thinking, as it enhances understanding, fosters collaboration, and improves decision-making. By fully engaging with the speaker, asking clarifying questions, and reflecting on their message, we gather diverse perspectives and accurate information — key components of effective analysis and evaluation. This reduces miscommunication and ensures well-informed judgments.

In problem-solving, active listening helps identify root causes and explore innovative solutions by valuing all viewpoints. It builds trust and empathy, creating a safe space for open dialogue, essential for resolving conflicts and making ethical decisions. For leaders and teams, active listening promotes inclusivity, ensuring everyone's voice is heard and contributing to more robust, collaborative outcomes.

Active listening also supports continuous learning, a critical aspect of critical thinking. By absorbing insights from others, we challenge assumptions, expand our knowledge, and refine our reasoning. It encourages self-reflection, helping us recognize biases and improve our thought processes.

In a world filled with information overload and rapid change, active listening ensures we remain adaptable, empathetic, and thoughtful. It strengthens our ability to think critically, solve problems effectively, and build meaningful connections. By practicing active listening, we enhance our critical thinking skills and contribute to a more understanding, innovative, and resilient world.

COLLABORATE WITH OTHERS

Collaboration is essential for effective critical thinking because it brings diverse perspectives, enhances problem-solving, and improves decision-making. Working with others' challenges, and assumptions uncovers blind spots and generates innovative solutions by pooling knowledge and expertise. For example, a team with varied backgrounds can approach problems from multiple angles, leading to more comprehensive outcomes.

Collaboration fosters learning and growth as individuals gain new insights and refine their thinking through discussions and debates. It increases accountability, encourages rigorous and disciplined analysis, and helps resolve conflicts by promoting open dialogue and mutual understanding. By considering multiple viewpoints, teams can make balanced, well-informed decisions.

Moreover, collaboration drives innovation and creativity by encouraging the free exchange of ideas and constructive debate. It builds trust and strengthens relationships, creating a supportive environment where critical thinking thrives. In an interconnected and complex world, collaboration is not just valuable — it is necessary to leverage critical thinking to achieve success, solve problems, and drive meaningful progress.

Applying and practicing critical thinking daily is essential for navigating life's complexities and making informed decisions. It helps us evaluate evidence, solve problems effectively, and avoid misinformation by questioning assumptions and verifying facts. Daily critical thinking fosters creativity and innovation by encouraging us to challenge the status quo and explore new ideas. It also builds resilience, enabling us to learn from setbacks and adapt to change.

Critical thinking enhances our ability to articulate ideas clearly, support arguments with evidence, and understand others' perspectives, improving relationships and teamwork. It also promotes ethical behavior by helping us consider the moral implications of our actions and align decisions with our values.

On a personal level, critical thinking encourages self-reflection, continuous learning, and growth. In professional settings, it drives success by improving problem-solving, decision-making, and strategic thinking. In a world filled with information overload and rapid change, daily critical thinking is necessary for making thoughtful choices, overcoming challenges, and thriving in both personal and professional life.

Chapter 2

TOOLS FOR CRITICAL THINKING

Critical thinking can be significantly enhanced by using specific **tools and frameworks** that provide structure and clarity to the thought process. These tools help analyze problems, evaluate information, and make well-reasoned decisions. Below are some of the more effective tools for critical thinking.

5 WHYS

The 5 Whys is a root cause analysis method that starts with identifying a problem and then iteratively asking, "Why did this happen?" With each answer, you ask "Why?" again until you uncover the underlying cause of an issue. Although commonly referred to as "5 Whys," the number is not fixed; you may need more or fewer iterations depending on the complexity of the problem.

HOW IT WORKS

- Identify the problem clearly.
- Ask the first "Why?" to determine the immediate cause.

- For each answer given, ask another "Why?" to understand what caused that factor.

- Continue until you arrive at the root cause – the point where asking "Why?" no longer yields a deeper explanation.

ITS SIGNIFICANCE

- **Simplicity:** It provides a straightforward, easy-to-understand method that does not require statistical analysis or complex tools.

- **Clarity:** Digging beneath the surface of symptoms helps organizations or individuals discover the true underlying issues rather than just treating superficial symptoms.

- **Improved Problem-Solving:** Uncovering the root cause allows for more effective corrective actions, which can prevent the problem from recurrence.

- **Versatility:** It is widely used in various fields such as manufacturing, software development, healthcare, and business processes.

- **Encourages Critical Thinking:** The iterative questioning technique promotes a culture of inquiry and continuous improvement, a core aspect of methodologies like Lean and Six Sigma.

The 5 Whys technique is significant because it helps teams quickly and efficiently identify the root cause of problems, better understand underlying issues, and implement corrective actions that lead to more sustainable improvements.

6 THINKING HATS

The **Six Thinking Hats** is a powerful critical thinking framework developed by Dr. Edward de Bono. It encourages individuals and teams to approach problems or decisions from six distinct perspectives, symbolized by six colored "hats." Each hat represents a different mode of thinking, helping to structure discussions, reduce conflict, and explore ideas comprehensively.

Each "hat" represents a specific type of thinking. By metaphorically "wearing" one hat at a time, individuals or groups can focus on one perspective without mixing emotions, facts, or creativity, often leading to clearer and more productive discussions.

THE SIX HATS AND THEIR ROLES

WHITE HAT *(Facts and Information)*

- Focus: Neutral and objective thinking.
- Questions to Ask:
  - What information do we have?
  - What information is missing?
  - What do the facts tell us?
- Example: Analyzing data or research to understand a situation.

RED HAT *(Emotions and Intuition)*

- Focus: Feelings, instincts, and gut reactions.
- Questions to Ask:

- How do I feel about this?
  - What is my intuition telling me?
- Example: Sharing emotional responses to a proposed change

BLACK HAT *(Critical Judgment)*

- Focus: Identifying risks, problems, and potential pitfalls.
- Questions to Ask:
  - What could go wrong?
  - What are the weaknesses of this idea?
- Example: Highlighting potential risks in a new business strategy.

YELLOW HAT *(Optimism and Benefits)*

- Focus: Positive thinking and exploring benefits.
- Questions to Ask:
  - What are the advantages of this idea?
  - What opportunities does this create?
- Example: Identifying the potential benefits of a new product launch.

GREEN HAT *(Creativity and New Ideas)*

- Focus: Generating creative solutions and alternatives.
- Questions to Ask:
  - What new ideas can we explore?
  - How can we improve this?
- Example: Brainstorming innovative ways to solve a problem.

BLUE HAT *(Process Control)*

- Focus: Managing the thinking process and summarizing findings.
- Questions to Ask:
  - What is our goal?
  - What have we learned so far?
  - What are the next steps?
- Example: A facilitator guiding the discussion and ensuring all hats are used effectively.

HOW IT WORKS

1. **Define the Problem or Goal**: Clearly state the issue or decision to be addressed.

2. **Assign the Hats**: Decide the order in which the hats will be used. For example:

   a. Start with the **White Hat** to gather facts.

   b. Use the **Red Hat** to explore emotions.

   c. Switch to the **Black Hat** to identify risks.

   d. Move to the **Yellow Hat** to explore benefits.

   e. Use the **Green Hat** to generate creative solutions.

   f. End with the **Blue Hat** to summarize and plan the next steps.

3. **Discuss Each Perspective**: Focus on one hat at a time, ensuring everyone contributes from that perspective.

4. **Summarize and Decide**: Use the **Blue Hat** to review insights and make informed decisions.

ITS SIGNIFICANCE

- **Structured Thinking**: Provides a clear framework for exploring problems and decisions, ensuring all perspectives are considered.

- **Reduces Conflict**: Separating emotions (Red Hat) from critical judgment (Black Hat) minimizes arguments and fosters collaboration.

- **Encourages Creativity**: The **Green Hat** ensures that creative ideas are given space and attention, leading to innovative solutions.

- **Balanced Decision-Making**: Combines facts (White Hat), risks (Black Hat), and benefits (Yellow Hat) to create well-rounded decisions.

- **Improves Communication**: Encourages participants to focus on one perspective at a time, reducing confusion and enhancing clarity.

- **Saves Time**: Organizing discussions into distinct modes of thinking prevents tangents and keeps meetings productive.

- **Enhances Team Collaboration**: Ensures everyone's voice is heard, as each hat provides a specific role for participants to contribute.

The Six Thinking Hats method is a versatile and effective critical thinking, problem-solving, and decision-making tool. Systematically exploring different perspectives ensures thorough analysis, reduces conflict, and fosters creativity. Whether used individually or in teams, this framework helps structure thinking, improve communication, and make balanced, well-informed decisions. Its significance lies in its ability to bring clarity, collaboration, and innovation to complex challenges.

SOCRATIC QUESTIONING METHOD

The **Socratic Questioning Method** is a form of disciplined questioning used to explore complex ideas, uncover assumptions, and stimulate critical thinking. Named after the ancient Greek philosopher Socrates, this method involves asking thought-provoking questions to challenge beliefs, clarify concepts, and arrive at a deeper understanding of truth. It is widely used in education, counseling, and problem-solving contexts.

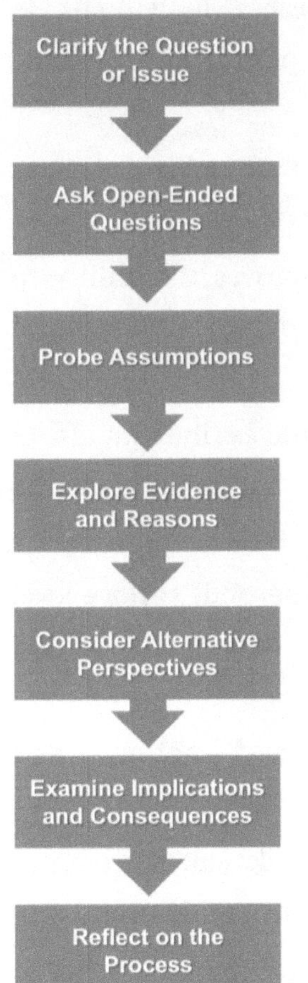

- Begin by identifying the topic or problem to explore.
- Example: *What does it mean to be a good leader?*

- Use questions that cannot be answered with a simple "yes" or "no."
- Example: *How would you define leadership?*

- Challenge underlying beliefs or assumptions.
- Example: *Why do you think leaders need to be charismatic?*

- Encourage the participant to provide evidence or reasoning for their views.
- Example: *What examples support your definition of leadership?*

- Ask questions that invite the participant to consider other viewpoints.
- Example: *How might someone with a different cultural background view leadership?*

- Explore the potential outcomes of a belief or decision.
- Example: *What might happen if leaders focused only on results and not on team morale?*

- Encourage the participant to reflect on their thinking and learning.
- Example: *How has this discussion changed your understanding of leadership?*

HOW IT WORKS

The Socratic Method is a dialogue-driven approach in which the questioner (often a teacher, mentor, or facilitator) guides participants through carefully crafted questions to examine their own thinking. The goal is not to provide answers but to encourage self-discovery and critical reflection.

ITS SIGNIFICANCE

- **Promotes Critical Thinking**: Encourages individuals to analyze their beliefs, question assumptions, and evaluate evidence.

- **Fosters Self-Discovery**: Helps participants arrive at their conclusions rather than relying on external answers.

- **Enhances Communication Skills**: Improves the ability to articulate thoughts, listen actively, and engage in meaningful dialogue.

- **Builds Intellectual Humility**: Encourages individuals to recognize the limits of their knowledge and remain open to new ideas.

- **Encourages Deep Learning**: Moves beyond surface-level understanding to explore the "why" and "how" behind concepts.

- **Reduces Bias**: Challenges preconceived notions and encourages consideration of alternative viewpoints.

- **Improves Problem-Solving**: Helps break down complex problems into manageable parts and explore multiple solutions.

- **Empowers Individuals**: Builds confidence in one's ability to think independently and critically.

The Socratic Questioning Method is a powerful tool for fostering critical thinking, self-discovery, and meaningful dialogue. By asking probing questions and encouraging reflection, it helps individuals and groups uncover deeper insights, challenge assumptions, and arrive at well-reasoned conclusions. Its significance lies in its ability to promote intellectual growth, improve communication, and empower individuals to think independently and critically in both personal and professional contexts.

Chapter 3

BARRIERS TO CRITICAL THINKING

The post-COVID-19 world has introduced new challenges and complexities that can inhibit critical thinking. These barriers stem from the pandemic's rapid changes, uncertainties, and psychological impacts.

Some key barriers to critical thinking in the post-Covid-19 world include:

INFORMATION OVERLOAD AND MISINFORMATION

The pandemic has created an unprecedented flood of information, with news outlets, social media platforms, governments, and health organizations constantly sharing updates, guidelines, and opinions. While this abundance of information can be valuable, it has also led to a significant challenge: much of the information is conflicting, misleading, or outright false. This "infodemic" has made it increasingly difficult for individuals to discern credible sources from unreliable ones, creating confusion and undermining trust in authoritative voices. As a result, people may struggle to evaluate information accurately, leading to poor decision-making and the rapid spread of misinformation.

The consequences of this information overload are far-reaching. Misinformation about COVID-19, such as false claims about treatments, vaccines, or transmission methods, has caused harm by influencing people to make decisions that jeopardize their health and the health of others. For example, some individuals have refused vaccines or ignored public health guidelines based on inaccurate information, contributing to prolonged outbreaks and unnecessary suffering. Beyond health, misinformation has also fueled social and political divisions, eroded trust in institutions, and created a climate of fear and uncertainty.

To address this challenge, it is essential to educate individuals on how to identify credible sources and recognize misinformation. This education should focus on building critical thinking skills and media literacy, empowering people to navigate the complex information landscape confidently.

The pandemic has underscored the importance of media literacy and critical thinking in an age of information overload. By equipping individuals with the skills to identify credible sources and recognize misinformation, we can empower them to make better decisions, protect their health, and contribute to a more informed and resilient society. In a world where misinformation can spread faster than the truth, education is our most powerful tool for combating its harmful effects.

INCREASED STRESS AND ANXIETY

The pandemic has not only posed physical health risks but has also taken a significant toll on mental health. Widespread stress, anxiety, and mental fatigue have become pervasive as people grapple with uncertainty, isolation, financial instability, and the constant barrage of alarming news. These psychological challenges can impair cognitive functions, making it harder for individuals to think, analyze information, and make reasoned decisions. When stress levels are high, the brain's ability to process information, focus, and solve problems is compromised, leading to poorer judgment and decision-making.

For example, chronic stress triggers the release of cortisol, a hormone that, in excess, can interfere with memory, attention, and executive functioning. Anxiety can narrow an individual's focus, causing them to fixate on perceived threats rather than considering the bigger picture. Mental fatigue, often resulting from prolonged stress or information overload, can lead to burnout, reducing motivation and the ability to engage in critical thinking. Collectively, these effects create a cycle where stress impairs cognitive function, which in turn exacerbates stress, further diminishing mental clarity and decision-making capabilities.

In the workplace, this can manifest as decreased productivity, increased errors, and poor strategic decisions. Employees struggling with stress and anxiety may find it difficult to concentrate, collaborate effectively, or innovate. Leaders, too, may struggle to navigate complex challenges and make sound decisions under pressure. On a broader scale, impaired cognitive function can affect how individuals interpret information, making them more susceptible to misinformation and less capable of evaluating risks and benefits accurately.

There is an urgent need to provide resources and support for mental health to address these challenges. By reducing stress and anxiety, individuals can regain their cognitive clarity, improve their critical thinking ability, and make informed decisions.

By prioritizing mental health and providing the necessary resources and support, organizations and communities can help individuals manage stress and anxiety more effectively. This, in turn, can restore cognitive function, enhance decision-making, and improve overall well-being. In a world where the pandemic has heightened uncertainty and complexity, supporting mental health is not just a moral imperative — it is a strategic necessity for building resilient individuals and organizations capable of thriving in challenging times.

RAPID TECHNOLOGICAL CHANGES

The rapid adoption of digital technologies, accelerated by the COVID-19 pandemic, has transformed how we work, communicate, and conduct business. While these advancements offer immense opportunities for efficiency, innovation, and growth, they have also created a steep learning curve for many individuals. Employees who were once comfortable with traditional tools and processes may now be overwhelmed by the influx of new software, platforms, and systems. This sense of overwhelm can hinder their ability to adapt, think critically about using these tools effectively, and fully leverage their potential.

For example, the shift to remote work necessitated the adoption of video conferencing tools, project management software, and cloud-based collaboration platforms — many of which were entirely new to a significant portion of the workforce. Similarly, healthcare, education, and retail industries have had to rapidly integrate digital solutions to meet changing demands. While some individuals embrace these changes, others may struggle to keep up, leading to frustration, resistance, and a decline in productivity. This gap in digital literacy can also stifle critical thinking, as employees may focus on simply navigating the tools rather than analyzing how to use them strategically to solve problems or improve outcomes.

To address this challenge, organizations must foster a culture of continuous learning that empowers employees to adapt confidently and competently to technological changes.

By fostering a culture of continuous learning, organizations can help employees overcome the challenges posed by rapid technological change. This enhances digital literacy and empowers individuals to think critically about how to use technology to drive innovation, solve problems, and achieve organizational goals. In a world where digital transformation is no longer optional but essential, continuous learning is key to building a resilient, adaptable, and future-ready workforce.

SOCIAL AND POLITICAL POLARIZATION

Again, the COVID-19 pandemic has been a public health crisis and a social and political one, deepening existing divides and creating new fault lines in societies worldwide. Lockdowns, economic hardships, and differing opinions on public health measures have fueled tensions, while the rapid spread of information — and misinformation — has further polarized communities. This environment has given rise to **echo chambers**, where individuals are primarily exposed to information and opinions that reinforce their existing beliefs, and **confirmation bias**, where people selectively interpret information to align with their preconceptions. As a result, many individuals have become less open to diverse perspectives and more likely to dismiss or attack information that contradicts their views.

This polarization has significant consequences for both individuals and organizations. The workplace can lead to strained relationships, reduced collaboration, and a lack of trust among team members. When employees are entrenched in their viewpoints, they may struggle to engage in constructive dialogue, solve problems collectively, or innovate effectively. On a broader scale, societal polarization can hinder progress on critical issues as people become more focused on defending their positions than finding common ground.

To counteract this trend, it is essential to encourage diverse perspectives and foster constructive debates. By actively encouraging diverse perspectives and constructive discussions, organizations and communities can counteract the effects of polarization and create a more collaborative and innovative culture. In a world where division often seems to dominate, fostering openness and mutual understanding is not just a moral imperative but a practical necessity for solving complex problems and building a more resilient society. Encouraging individuals to step out of their echo chambers and engage with differing viewpoints can lead to better decision-making, stronger relationships, and a more united future.

ECONOMIC UNCERTAINTY

Economic instability and job insecurity have become defining features of the modern business landscape, exacerbated by global events such as the COVID-19 pandemic, geopolitical tensions, and rapid technological changes. This climate of uncertainty and fear profoundly affects both individuals and organizations. Financial stress can dominate employees' thoughts, narrowing their focus to immediate concerns and reducing their capacity for long-term, strategic thinking. When individuals are preoccupied with worries about job security, paying bills, or managing debt, they are less able to engage in creative problem-solving, innovation, or planning. This, in turn, can stifle organizational growth and resilience.

Economic instability also poses significant challenges for organizations. Uncertainty can lead to reduced consumer spending, disrupted supply chains, and volatile markets, making planning and executing long-term strategies difficult. Additionally, a workforce stressed and distracted by financial concerns is less productive, less engaged, and more likely to experience burnout. This creates a vicious cycle where economic instability undermines employee well-being, which in turn hampers organizational performance, further exacerbating economic challenges.

To break this cycle and foster sustained growth, organizations must take proactive steps to reduce economic uncertainty and financially stabilize their employees. By adopting that, organizations can create a more stable and supportive environment for their employees, reducing financial stress and fostering a culture of long-term, strategic thinking. When employees feel secure and valued, they are more likely to contribute their best work, driving innovation and growth for the organization. In a world where economic uncertainty is often the norm, providing financial stability is not just a compassionate choice but a strategic imperative for building a resilient and thriving workforce.

REMOTE WORK CHALLENGES

The shift to remote work, accelerated by the COVID-19 pandemic, has fundamentally transformed how teams communicate and collaborate. While remote work offers numerous benefits, such as flexibility and access to a global talent pool, it has also disrupted traditional methods of interaction that many organizations relied on for decades. The absence of face-to-face communication can lead to misunderstandings, as nuances like tone, body language, and context are often lost in virtual exchanges. This can reduce team cohesion, as employees may feel isolated or disconnected from their colleagues. Collaborative problem-solving becomes more challenging when team members cannot easily gather around a whiteboard or engage in spontaneous brainstorming sessions.

These challenges highlight the urgent need for organizations to develop and implement effective communication and collaboration tools tailored to remote teams. Remote work can hinder productivity, innovation, and employee satisfaction without the right tools and strategies.

The shift to remote work is not just a temporary response to the pandemic but a long-term workplace transformation. As organizations adapt to this new reality, developing effective communication and collaboration tools for remote teams becomes necessary. By investing in the right tools, establishing clear guidelines, and fostering a culture of openness and connection, organizations can overcome the challenges of remote work and unlock its full potential. In doing so, they can create a more flexible, inclusive, and productive work environment that benefits employees and the organization.

COGNITIVE BIASES

The pandemic has disrupted daily life and amplified certain cognitive biases that influence how people perceive information, make decisions, and interact with others. In times of crisis, the human brain often relies on mental shortcuts to quickly process overwhelming amounts of information. While these shortcuts can be helpful, they can also lead to distorted perceptions and flawed judgments. Three cognitive biases that have become particularly pronounced during the pandemic are **fear-based decision-making**, **negative bias**, and **herd mentality**. These biases can have significant consequences for individuals and society, often leading to irrational decisions and actions.

Fear is a powerful emotion that can override rational thinking. During the pandemic, the constant stream of alarming news, uncertainty about the future, and concerns about health and safety have heightened fear levels. This fear can lead to **risk aversion** or **overreaction**, where individuals make decisions based on emotion rather than logic.

Negative bias refers to the tendency to focus more on negative information than positive information. During the pandemic, this bias has been fueled by the prevalence of bad news, such as rising case numbers, economic downturns, and social unrest. Negative bias can lead to a distorted view of reality, where individuals underestimate positive developments or overlook potential solutions.

Herd mentality, or the tendency to follow the actions or opinions of a group, has also been amplified during the pandemic. In uncertain times, people often look to others for cues on how to behave, leading to behaviors like panic buying, vaccine hesitancy, or the spread of misinformation. Herd mentality can create a feedback loop, where irrational actions by a few individuals influence the behavior of many, often with harmful consequences.

These cognitive biases can distort perception and judgment, leading to irrational decisions and actions. On an individual level, this can result in poor health choices, financial mistakes, or strained relationships. Societally, it can exacerbate public health crises, economic instability, and social divisions. These biases can hinder effective decision-making, reduce innovation, and create a culture of fear or conformity in the workplace.

By promoting self-awareness, we can help them make more rational, informed decisions — even in times of crisis. This benefits individuals and contributes to a more resilient, thoughtful, and collaborative society. In a world where uncertainty and complexity are the norm, understanding and addressing cognitive biases is critical to building a better future.

HEALTH CONCERNS

Ongoing health concerns related to COVID-19, such as long-term effects and new variants, create persistent anxiety. **The** constant worry about health can distract from other important issues and reduce mental bandwidth for critical thinking. We must ensure access to healthcare and promote healthy lifestyles to alleviate health concerns.

BURNOUT AND FATIGUE

The prolonged nature of the COVID-19 pandemic has taken a significant toll on individuals worldwide, leading to widespread burnout and fatigue. The constant stress of adapting to new norms, managing health risks, and balancing personal and professional responsibilities has left many people feeling physically, emotionally, and mentally drained. This exhaustion can severely impair cognitive functions, making concentrating, analyzing information, and making thoughtful decisions difficult. In the workplace, burnout and fatigue can lead to decreased productivity, increased errors, and a decline in overall morale. To address these challenges, organizations must take proactive steps to encourage work life balance and provide support for managing fatigue.

In a world where the lines between work and personal life have become increasingly blurred, prioritizing employee well-being is not just a moral imperative but a strategic necessity. Organizations that invest in creating a supportive and balanced work environment will be better positioned to navigate the challenges of the pandemic and build a resilient, thriving workforce for the future.

By addressing these barriers, individuals and organizations can foster a more conducive environment for critical thinking, enabling better decision-making and problem-solving in the post-COVID-19 world.

3.1 TIME TO REFLECT

Here are some key points to reflect on to enhance and practice these elements of critical thinking effectively.

Clarity: Ensure you understand the problem and explain your ideas clearly, so everyone understands.

- *Use examples or stories to illustrate your point for better clarity.*

Accuracy: Check that your information is correct to make smart decisions.

- *Double-check important details to avoid errors in reasoning.*

Precision: Be specific in your thoughts and avoid using unclear language to prevent confusion.

- *Break down complex ideas into smaller parts to communicate more precisely.*

Relevance: Focus on what truly matters and ignore unnecessary details for better decision-making

- *Prioritize tasks based on their importance to stay focused on what is relevant.*

Depth: Look deeper into information to understand the hidden meanings and complexities.

- *Ask "why" multiple times to uncover more profound insights into a problem.*

Logic: Use logical reasoning to evaluate arguments and reach valid conclusions.

- *Create a step-by-step plan to approach and solve a problem logically.*

Significance: Identify the most crucial aspects of a problem and tackle them first.

- *Set clear goals to measure the significance of each task in reaching a solution.*

Fairness: Keep an open mind, consider different viewpoints, and avoid biases in your analysis.

- *Seek feedback from others to ensure fairness in your decision-making process.*

Creativity: Think creatively to develop unique solutions and look at problems from new angles.

- *Brainstorm with others to gather diverse perspectives and stimulate creative thinking.*

Regularly reflecting on these points can sharpen your critical thinking skills, make better decisions, and approach problems with greater clarity and confidence.

PART 2

THE ART OF ADAPTIVE THINKING

"Intelligence is the ability to adapt to change."

– Stephen Hawking

In today's fast-paced world, change is the only constant. Whether it is in your personal life or professional environment, the ability to adapt is crucial. This is where **adaptive thinking** comes into play. It is not just a skill but a mindset that enables you to navigate uncertainty and respond effectively to new challenges.

Adaptive thinking recognizes unexpected situations, evaluates possible responses, and makes informed decisions. It is not simply about survival but about thriving in an ever-changing landscape.

The art of adaptive thinking is a vital skill in today's fast-paced, ever-changing world. It empowers individuals and organizations to navigate uncertainty, solve complex problems, and innovate effectively. Adaptive thinkers can thrive in dynamic environments by cultivating flexibility, creativity, and resilience, turning challenges into opportunities for growth and success. In a world where change is the only constant, adaptive thinking is not just critical — it is essential.

Chapter 4

THE BEST WAY TO DEALING WITH UNEXPECTED SITUATIONS

4.1 WHAT IS ADPATIVE THINKING

Adaptive thinking is the ability to adjust one's thought processes, strategies, and behaviors in response to changing circumstances, unexpected challenges, or new information. It involves flexibility, creativity, and resilience, enabling individuals to navigate uncertainty, solve complex problems, and thrive in dynamic environments.

Adaptive thinking is not just about solving problems but about thriving in dynamic environments by embracing change and learning from experiences. Unlike reactive approaches, adaptive thinking is proactive, anticipating and embracing change to achieve better outcomes. Adaptive thinking is essential for staying relevant, innovative, and resilient in a rapidly changing world marked by technological advancements, economic shifts, and global challenges. It empowers individuals to break down complex issues, explore multiple solutions, and learn from setbacks, fostering personal and professional growth. It drives agility, innovation, and long-term success for organizations by enabling them to respond effectively to market shifts and emerging trends. By cultivating a curiosity, openness, and continuous learning mindset, adaptive thinkers turn challenges into opportunities, ensuring they remain competitive and impactful in an ever-evolving world. Adaptive thinking is not just a skill but a necessity for thriving in today's fast-paced, interconnected environment.

Adaptive thinking is characterized by several key traits that enable individuals to thrive in dynamic and uncertain environments.

Flexibility is the ability to shift perspectives, approaches, or plans when faced with new information or obstacles, allowing for quick adjustments to changing circumstances. Adopted in adaptive thinking is like being a **mental gymnast** — it is the ability to bend and stretch your thoughts, plans, and actions when things do not go as expected. Imagine you are planning a picnic, but it starts raining; instead of giving up, you quickly shift to an indoor plan, like having a cozy movie day. That is flexibility in action. In adaptive thinking, flexibility means being open to change, willing to let go of old ideas, and ready to try new approaches when the situation demands it. It is about staying calm and resourceful when faced with surprises, whether at work, in relationships, or everyday life. For example, if a project at work hits a snag, a flexible thinker does not panic — they brainstorm new solutions, adjust their strategy, and keep moving forward. In short, flexibility is the superpower that helps you roll with the punches and turn challenges into opportunities.

Creativity involves thinking beyond conventional boundaries, enabling individuals to explore new perspectives and generate unique solutions. Creativity fosters innovation by stepping outside the traditional way of doing things, allowing new ideas to emerge that may not be immediately obvious through standard approaches. This process encourages individuals or teams to break free from established patterns, consider alternative possibilities, and create original strategies, products, or services. As a result, creativity becomes a key driver of problem-solving, helping to find effective and unconventional ways to overcome obstacles or meet evolving needs. Whether in business, technology, or any field, creativity leads to fresh thinking, facilitates adaptation to change, and drives continuous improvement, making it an essential tool for growth and success in today's rapidly evolving world.

Resilience is the ability to bounce back from adversity, setbacks, or difficulties without losing momentum or focus on long-term goals. It involves maintaining a positive mindset, even when faced with obstacles, and finding ways to adapt and overcome challenges. Resilient individuals or organizations do not get discouraged by failures; instead, they view them as learning opportunities and continue working toward their objectives. This capacity to recover quickly allows them to stay persistent and committed, regardless of their difficulties. Resilience also enables people to manage stress effectively, adjust to changing circumstances, and keep moving forward in uncertainty, ultimately driving progress and success. In both personal and professional contexts, resilience fosters perseverance, ensuring that individuals or teams stay on track, even when faced with unexpected hurdles or prolonged hardships.

Open-mindedness is the willingness to embrace new ideas, perspectives, and feedback, even when they challenge existing beliefs or ways of thinking. It involves being receptive to diverse viewpoints, acknowledging that there may be alternative solutions or approaches that can lead to better outcomes. By cultivating open-mindedness, individuals foster an environment of inclusivity where everyone feels valued and heard, leading to stronger collaboration within teams or organizations. This openness encourages creativity and innovation, as people are likelier to contribute their unique ideas without fear of judgment. Additionally, open-mindedness enhances problem-solving by allowing individuals to consider broader possibilities, making it easier to adapt to change and make more informed decisions. In both personal and professional settings, open-mindedness promotes constructive dialogue, fosters mutual respect, and supports continuous learning, ensuring growth and development occur within a dynamic and supportive environment.

Proactive learning is actively and continuously seeking new knowledge, skills, and experiences to stay ahead of emerging trends and changes in any field. It involves taking the initiative to anticipate future challenges or opportunities rather than waiting for them to arise. By engaging in proactive learning, individuals position themselves to adapt to new environments, technologies, or strategies, ensuring they remain competitive and relevant. This approach encourages a mindset of lifelong learning, where personal and professional growth becomes a continuous process. It also promotes adaptability, as those actively seeking to learn are better equipped to adjust to unforeseen circumstances, navigate uncertainties, and address complex problems. Proactive learning fosters resilience and agility, allowing individuals to thrive in dynamic environments and continuously improve their performance, ensuring long-term success and development.

Finally, **situational awareness** is the ability to assess and understand a given situation's context, environment, and dynamics, allowing individuals to make well-informed decisions based on current circumstances. It involves observing the immediate and long-term factors at play, such as the behavior of people, changes in external conditions, and emerging trends, ensuring that decisions are timely and relevant. Individuals can better anticipate challenges and identify opportunities by cultivating situational awareness, allowing them to respond proactively and strategically to complex and evolving scenarios. When combined with other skills, such as critical thinking, adaptability, and resilience, situational awareness forms the foundation of **adaptive thinking**. This mindset enables individuals to remain agile in the face of uncertainty. This empowers them to adjust their approach, solve problems creatively, and make decisions that lead to positive outcomes, even in fast-changing or unpredictable environments. This ability is crucial for navigating complexities, fostering innovation, and achieving success in today's rapidly evolving world.

4.2 THE DISSIMILARITY BETWEEN ADAPTIVE THINKING AND CRITICAL THINKING

While adaptive thinking and critical thinking are essential cognitive skills, they serve distinct purposes and operate in different contexts. Let us examine their polarity and what makes each distinctive.

Firstly, adaptive thinking focuses on flexibility, creativity, and resilience in response to changing or uncertain situations. It emphasizes adjusting strategies, behaviors and thought processes to navigate dynamic and unpredictable environments. For example, a business leader might use adaptive thinking to pivot their company's operations during a crisis, such as shifting to remote work or adopting new technologies to meet evolving customer needs. This type of thinking is particularly valuable in fast-paced or volatile contexts where traditional approaches may no longer be effective.

On the other hand, critical thinking focuses on analyzing, evaluating, and synthesizing information to make reasoned judgments or decisions. It emphasizes logical reasoning, evidence-based analysis, and structured problem-solving. For instance, a manager might use critical thinking to assess the pros and cons of a new policy, evaluate data to identify trends or determine the validity of an argument. Critical thinking is essential in situations that require careful examination, such as scientific research, strategic planning, or ethical decision-making.

While adaptive thinking involves responding to change with agility and innovation, critical thinking involves **understanding and solving problems** through systematic analysis and evidence-based reasoning. These skills enable individuals to navigate complexity, make informed decisions, and thrive in stable and dynamic environments. Adaptive thinking ensures flexibility and resilience in uncertainty, while critical thinking ensures accuracy and clarity in understanding and addressing challenges.

Adaptive thinking aims to thrive in unpredictable or rapidly changing environments by being flexible and innovative. It aims to enable individuals and organizations to respond effectively to new challenges, opportunities, or disruptions, ensuring they can adapt and succeed even when circumstances shift unexpectedly. For example, during a global crisis like the COVID-19 pandemic, adaptive thinking allowed businesses to pivot to remote work, adopt new technologies, and find creative ways to serve customers. This type of thinking is particularly valuable in dynamic fields such as entrepreneurship, technology, and crisis management, where the ability to adjust quickly is crucial for survival and growth.

In contrast, **critical thinking** aims to solve problems, make informed decisions, and evaluate the validity of arguments or information. Its purpose is to ensure that decisions are based on logical reasoning, thorough analysis, and credible evidence. Critical thinking focuses on understanding the root causes of issues, assessing the strengths and weaknesses of different perspectives, and arriving at well-reasoned conclusions. For instance, scientists use critical thinking to design experiments, analyze data, and draw valid conclusions. In contrast, a manager might use it to evaluate a new business strategy's potential risks and benefits. This skill is essential in fields like science, law, education, and strategic planning, where accuracy, clarity, and validity are paramount.

While adaptive thinking is about **thriving in uncertainty** by embracing change and innovation, critical thinking solves **problems** through structured analysis and evidence-based reasoning. These skills complement each other: critical thinking provides the foundation for understanding and analyzing a problem, while adaptive thinking enables flexible and creative responses to that problem. This combination ensures that individuals and organizations can address challenges effectively and adapt and innovate in the face of change.

Adaptive thinking is used in dynamic, uncertain, or rapidly changing situations where traditional approaches may not work. It is particularly valuable in environments that require quick adjustments, creative problem-solving, and the ability to pivot strategies in response to new information or unexpected challenges. For example, in **entrepreneurship**, adaptive thinking helps startups navigate market shifts, experiment with new business models, and seize emerging opportunities. In **crisis management**, it enables leaders to respond effectively to emergencies, such as natural disasters or economic downturns, by developing flexible and innovative solutions.

Similarly, in **innovation-driven fields** like technology and design, adaptive thinking fosters the development of groundbreaking products and services by encouraging experimentation and iteration.

On the other hand, **critical thinking** is used in situations that require careful analysis, evaluation, and decision-making. It is essential in contexts where accuracy, logic, and evidence-based reasoning are paramount.

For instance,

- In **science**, critical thinking is used to design experiments, analyze data, and draw valid conclusions.

- In **law**, it helps lawyers evaluate evidence, construct arguments, and interpret complex regulations.

- In **education**, critical thinking enables students and educators to analyze texts, solve problems, and engage in meaningful discussions.

- Strategic planning allows leaders to assess risks, weigh alternatives, and make informed decisions that align with long-term goals.

While adaptive thinking thrives in **fluid and unpredictable environments**, critical thinking excels in **structured and analytical contexts**. Together, these skills ensure that individuals and organizations can respond effectively to change and make well-reasoned decisions that stand up to scrutiny. For example, a business leader might use critical thinking to analyze market trends and develop a strategic plan while relying on adaptive thinking to adjust that plan as new challenges or opportunities arise. This combination of skills is essential for success in a world that demands flexibility and precision.

Adaptive thinking focuses on experimenting, iterating, and adapting solutions in real time. It embraces a trial-and-error approach, where individuals test different strategies, learn from failures, and refine their methods as new information or circumstances arise. This approach is particularly practical in dynamic or uncertain environments, where rigid plans may not work, and flexibility is key. For example, a tech startup might use adaptive thinking to develop a new app by releasing a prototype, gathering user feedback, and making continuous improvements based on real-world usage. Adaptive thinkers are comfortable with ambiguity and view setbacks as opportunities to learn and grow, allowing them to pivot quickly and find innovative solutions to emerging challenges.

In contrast, **critical thinking** focuses on systematic analysis, evidence-based reasoning, and logical problem-solving. It emphasizes a structured approach to understanding problems, evaluating options, and making decisions. Critical thinkers gather and assess relevant information, identify patterns, and weigh the pros and cons of different solutions before concluding. For instance, a scientist might use critical thinking to design a controlled experiment, analyze the results, and draw valid conclusions based on the data. Similarly, a business leader might use critical thinking to evaluate a new investment opportunity's potential risks and benefits before deciding. This method ensures that decisions are well-reasoned, thorough, and based on solid evidence.

While adaptive thinking is about **flexibility and real time adaptation**, critical thinking is **precision and thorough evaluation**. Together, these approaches complement each other: critical thinking provides the foundation for understanding and analyzing a problem. In contrast, adaptive thinking enables the flexibility to adjust and innovate as new information or challenges arise. For example, a company might use critical thinking to develop a strategic plan and adaptive thinking to modify that plan in response to changing market conditions. This combination ensures that individuals and organizations can address problems effectively while remaining agile and responsive in a rapidly changing world.

Adaptive thinking leads to innovative, flexible, and context-specific solutions that are tailored to the unique demands of a situation. By embracing experimentation and iteration, adaptive thinkers can develop creative approaches that address emerging challenges and capitalize on new opportunities. This ability to adapt ensures that individuals and organizations can thrive in environments characterized by uncertainty and change. For example, during the COVID-19 pandemic, businesses that used adaptive thinking could pivot to remote work, develop new products, and find innovative ways to serve customers, ensuring their survival and growth despite unprecedented disruptions. Adaptive thinking fosters resilience and agility, enabling individuals and organizations to navigate complexity and remain competitive in a rapidly evolving world.

On the other hand, **critical thinking** leads to well-reasoned, evidence-based decisions that are grounded in logic and thorough analysis. Critical thinkers ensure that their conclusions are accurate, clear, and valid by systematically evaluating information, identifying patterns, and weighing alternatives. This approach is essential for solving complex problems, making informed decisions, and avoiding errors or biases. For instance, a scientist using critical thinking can draw reliable conclusions from experimental data, while a manager can make strategic decisions based on a careful assessment of risks and benefits. Critical thinking ensures that decisions are effective, defensible, and aligned with long-term goals.

While adaptive thinking focuses on **innovation and flexibility**, critical thinking emphasizes **accuracy and validity**. Together, these outcomes complement each other: critical thinking provides the foundation for making sound decisions, while adaptive thinking enables the flexibility to adjust and innovate as circumstances change. For example, a company might use critical thinking to develop a well-researched business strategy and adaptive thinking to refine that strategy in response to shifting market conditions. This combination ensures that individuals and organizations can achieve short-term adaptability and long-term success in an ever-changing world.

Finally, the key characteristics of adaptive and critical thinking differ. **Adaptive thinking is about responding to change and thriving in unpredictable environments, while critical thinking is about understanding and solving problems through structured reasoning.**

ADAPTIVE THINKING

- **Flexibility:** The ability of an individual or organization to shift perspectives or approaches when needed.

- **Creativity:** How an individual or organization generates innovative solutions to novel problems.

- **Resilience:** How quickly an individual or organization recovers from setbacks and maintains focus.

- **Open-Mindedness:** An individual or organization's willingness to consider new ideas and feedback.

CRITICAL THINKING

- **Analysis**: The ability of an individual or organization to break down complex information into smaller parts.

- **Evaluation**: How an individual or organization assesses the credibility and relevance of information.

- **Logic**: An individual or organization's ability to apply structured reasoning to conclude.

- **Reflection**: How an individual or organization reviews and improves one's thought processes.

Adaptive thinking and critical thinking are vital skills, but they serve different purposes. Adaptive thinking involves responding to change with flexibility and creativity, while critical thinking involves **analyzing and solving problems** with logic and evidence. Together, they enable individuals and organizations to navigate complexity, make informed decisions, and thrive in a rapidly changing world.

Chapter 5

DEVELOPING AN ADAPTIVE GROWTH MINDSET

Developing a growth mindset means believing you can improve your skills, intelligence, and abilities through effort, learning, and practice. It is like thinking of your brain as a muscle — the more you work it, the stronger it gets. Instead of seeing challenges as roadblocks, you see them as growth opportunities. For example, if you fail at something, you do not think, "I am just not good at this." Instead, you think, "What can I learn from this to improve next time?" A growth mindset also means staying curious and open to new ideas, like trying out a new hobby or learning a new skill, even if it initially feels hard. It is about valuing effort and persistence, knowing that success comes from practice, and not giving up. For instance, if you are struggling with a tough project at work, you keep trying different approaches until you find one that works. A growth mindset also involves seeking feedback and using it to improve rather than taking it personally. In short, it is about embracing change, learning from mistakes, and believing you can always improve. This mindset helps you stay flexible, resilient, and ready to tackle whatever life throws your way.

A **growth mindset** is the belief that abilities, intelligence, and skills can be developed through effort, learning, and persistence. In the context of **adaptive thinking**, developing a growth mindset is crucial because it empowers individuals to embrace change, learn from challenges, and continuously improve their ability to navigate uncertainty and complexity. It encourages individuals to see challenges as opportunities for growth rather than obstacles to avoid. Adaptive thinkers thrive in dynamic environments where challenges are inevitable. By viewing challenges as chances to learn and improve, they remain motivated and resilient, even when faced with setbacks. A business leader facing a sudden market shift sees it as an opportunity to innovate and explore new strategies rather than a threat to their existing model.

It also reframes failure as a valuable learning experience rather than a reflection of one's abilities. Adaptive thinkers understand that failure is a natural part of experimentation and innovation. They analyze what went wrong, extract lessons, and apply those insights to future efforts. A startup that fails to attract customers with its initial product uses the feedback to refine its offering and eventually succeeds.

A growth mindset emphasizes the importance of effort and persistence in achieving success. Adaptive thinkers are willing to work to adapt to new situations, even when progress is slow or difficult. They understand that mastery and resilience come from consistent effort. An employee learning a new software tool persists through the initial learning curve, eventually becoming proficient and more efficient.

A growth mindset involves actively seeking feedback and using it to improve. Adaptive thinkers value input from others and use it to refine their strategies and approaches. They are open to constructive criticism and see it as a tool for growth. They also foster curiosity and a willingness to explore new ideas and perspectives. Adaptive thinkers are naturally curious and open to learning. They seek new knowledge, skills, and experiences to stay ahead of change. In this way, they build emotional and mental resilience by focusing on progress and learning rather than fixed outcomes. They are resilient because they believe in improving and overcoming challenges. They bounce back from setbacks and remain focused on their goals.

Here are some points why a growth mindset is essential for adaptive thinking.

- It enhances flexibility as individuals are more willing to adapt and try new approaches.

- It helps individuals recover from setbacks and stay motivated in facing challenges.

- It encourages creativity and experimentation, leading to innovative solutions.

- It promotes lifelong learning by keeping individuals curious and committed to continuous improvement.

- It enables individuals to approach problems with a solution-oriented mindset.

5.1 EMBRACING CHANGE AND UNCERTAINTY

A **growth mindset** is the belief that abilities and intelligence can be developed through effort, learning, and persistence. This mindset fosters a positive, proactive approach to challenges, particularly when facing **change** and **uncertainty**. Rather than seeing these as obstacles or threats, individuals with a growth mindset see them as opportunities for **personal development, creativity,** and **innovation**. When combined with **adaptive thinking**, a growth mindset becomes a powerful tool for embracing change and uncertainty.

REFRAMING CHANGE AS AN OPPORTUNITY

The concept of mindset, particularly the distinction between fixed and growth mindsets, plays a critical role in how individuals approach change, challenges, and personal development. Coined by psychologist Carol Dweck, these mindsets describe people's underlying beliefs about their abilities and potential. While a **growth mindset** fosters resilience, adaptability, and a love for learning, a **fixed mindset** can limit personal and professional growth by creating barriers to embracing change and overcoming challenges. Understanding the differences between these mindsets is essential, especially in today's rapidly evolving world, where adaptability and continuous learning are key to success.

Individuals with a **fixed mindset** believe that their abilities, intelligence, and talents are static traits. Essentially, they think they are born with a certain level of capability and cannot change or improve significantly. This belief system shapes how they perceive and respond to change and challenges. Change is often seen as a threat rather than an opportunity for these individuals. They may feel anxious or overwhelmed when faced with new situations, fearing that they lack the skills or intelligence to adapt. This can lead to resistance to change, as they prefer to stay within their comfort zone where they feel secure.

Failure is particularly daunting for individuals with a fixed mindset. They view mistakes or setbacks as evidence of their inherent limitations, which can lead to a fear of taking risks or trying new things. This fear of failure can stifle creativity and innovation as they avoid challenges that might expose their perceived shortcomings. Because they believe their abilities are fixed, individuals with a fixed mindset often avoid challenges that might push them beyond their current capabilities. They may stick to tasks they know they can accomplish easily, missing out on opportunities for growth and development.

Those with a fixed mindset may become defensive or dismissive when confronted with criticism or feedback. They interpret constructive feedback as a personal attack on their abilities rather than an opportunity to improve.

In contrast, individuals with a **growth mindset** believe their abilities and intelligence can be developed through effort, learning, and persistence. This mindset empowers them to view change and challenges as opportunities rather than threats.

They understand that change is inevitable and see it as a chance to grow. Instead of feeling overwhelmed, they approach new situations with curiosity and a willingness to learn. They think, "This is an opportunity to expand my skills and gain new insights."

Failure is not seen as a reflection of their limitations but as a natural part of the learning process. Individuals with a growth mindset view setbacks as valuable feedback that can help them improve and grow. They are more likely to take risks and persevere in difficulties. A growth mindset encourages individuals to seek out challenges and step outside their comfort zone. They understand that tackling difficult tasks is essential for personal and professional development. This proactive approach fosters resilience and adaptability.

Those with a growth mindset are inspired by others' success and view it as an opportunity to learn. They are more likely to collaborate, share knowledge, and seek mentorship to further their development.

In a business environment, mindset plays a crucial role in shaping organizational culture, employee performance, and overall success. A workforce dominated by a fixed mindset may resist change, avoid innovation, and struggle to adapt to new challenges. On the other hand, a growth mindset fosters a culture of continuous learning, collaboration, and resilience, enabling organizations to thrive in the face of uncertainty.

For example, during the COVID-19 pandemic, companies with employees who embraced a growth mindset were better equipped to adapt to remote work, adopt new technologies, and navigate economic disruptions. These individuals viewed the pandemic's challenges as opportunities to learn new skills, improve processes, and innovate.

The difference between a fixed mindset and a growth mindset lies in how individuals perceive and respond to change and challenges. While a fixed mindset can lead to fear, resistance, and stagnation, a growth mindset empowers individuals to embrace change, learn from failure, and continuously improve. In today's fast-paced and ever-changing world, cultivating a growth mindset is essential for personal and professional success. By fostering a culture of learning, resilience, and adaptability, organizations can unlock the full potential of their workforce and thrive in the face of uncertainty.

LEARNING THROUGH FAILURE

One key aspect of a growth mindset is the understanding that failure is not permanent or debilitating. It is seen as feedback — a valuable learning tool that helps guide future decisions. When faced with failure, individuals with a growth mindset ask themselves, "What can I learn from this?" instead of "What is wrong with me?"

This mindset leads to innovation in environments like business, education, or sports because failure is not seen as the end of the road. Instead, mistakes are considered opportunities to experiment, revise approaches, and try different solutions. For example, a company could embrace customer feedback — even when it is negative — because it allows them to improve products and services.

EMBRACING UNCERTAINTY

Uncertainty can paralyze individuals who see it as a source of anxiety. On the other hand, those with a growth mindset view uncertainty as an inevitable part of **personal and professional growth**. When faced with uncertain situations, such as a new market, untested product, or innovative project, they understand that there is no clear roadmap, but that makes it exciting.

A growth mindset encourages exploration and risk-taking. Instead of waiting for the perfect solution or fearing failure, individuals are willing to step into the unknown, experiment with different approaches, and discover new opportunities. This is especially valuable in rapidly changing industries like retail or technology, where adapting and innovating is critical to staying competitive.

RESILIENCE AND PERSISTENCE

Change, especially if it is disruptive, often comes with challenges. However, a growth mindset builds resilience — the ability to persevere through difficulties. When faced with setbacks, individuals with a growth mindset do not give up easily. Instead, they focus on **finding solutions**, refining strategies, and continuing forward. This helps foster a **culture of persistence,** where challenges are seen as part of the growth process. Rather than being disheartened by obstacles, people with a growth mindset are energized by the prospect of **improvement**. They maintain a positive attitude and keep pushing forward, ultimately leading to long-term success. For example, when a company opens new stores in unfamiliar regions, it may face logistical or cultural challenges. A growth mindset helps them learn from mistakes and keep improving their approach.

Change, then, becomes a source of **creative energy**. Individuals or teams do not feel limited by what they know; instead, they are motivated to **think outside the box** and devise innovative solutions to new problems. This is essential in industries where differentiation and uniqueness are key.

ADAPTING TO RAPID CHANGE

In today's world, change is happening faster than ever. Whether it is shifts in customer expectations, technological advances, or market fluctuations, businesses need to be **agile**. A growth mindset helps individuals stay adaptable and agile, ensuring sudden changes do not throw them course. With a growth mindset, change becomes an ongoing process. Individuals do not just adapt once; they continuously learn, refine, and grow over time. For example, when a retailer needs to adapt to a new e-commerce platform or pivot due to a global crisis, those with a growth mindset quickly learn new skills, adapt their strategies, and lead the company through the transition.

A growth mindset reframes the **uncertainty** and **challenges** of change as **exciting opportunities for learning** and **innovation**. Instead of viewing obstacles as roadblocks, individuals with a growth mindset see them as *'stepping stones'* toward greater **personal development, creativity**, and **resilience**. This mindset fosters a **proactive, collaborative**, and **adaptable** approach to change, leading to greater success for individuals and organizations alike, which thrive on constant innovation and growth in a rapidly changing market.

5.2 REAL-WORLD EXAMPLES OF ADAPTIVE THINKING

Here are some real-world examples of adaptive thinking in business and personal life.

BUSINESS CONTEXT

PIVOTING BUSINESS MODELS

During the COVID-19 pandemic, many restaurants traditionally relied on dine-in customers quickly adapted to delivery and takeout services. Some even created meal kits for customers to cook at home.

Businesses recognize the need to change the business model to survive and thrive under new constraints.

REMOTE WORK TRANSITION

Companies like Twitter (now 'X') rapidly transitioned to remote work setups during the pandemic, implementing new technologies and policies to support their workforce.

Adapting to a new working method by leveraging technology and rethinking traditional office-based work structures.

PRODUCT INNOVATION

Netflix started as a DVD rental service but quickly adapted to the rise of digital streaming, becoming a leader in online content delivery.

The product offering is continuously evolving to meet changing consumer preferences and technological advancements.

PERSONAL LIFE CONTEXT

CAREER CHANGES

An individual who loses their job in a declining industry (e.g., traditional print media) might retrain in a growing field like digital marketing or data analysis.

Recognizing the need to acquire new skills and adapt to the changing job market is essential to adapting to an ever-changing world.

FINANCIAL MANAGEMENT

During economic downturns, individuals might adapt by cutting discretionary spending, finding additional income streams, or reallocating investments to more stable options.

Adjusting financial strategies to cope with economic uncertainty and protect personal finances.

PARENTING

Parents might adapt their parenting strategies as their children grow, shifting from direct supervision to fostering independence and responsibility.

Evolving parenting approaches to meet the changing needs and developmental stages of children.

5.3 TOOLS FOR ADAPTIVE THINKING

Adaptive thinking is the ability to adjust one's thinking, behavior, and approach in response to changing conditions or unexpected challenges. It is essential for problem-solving, creativity, and decision-making, especially in complex or uncertain environments. Several tools and techniques can help develop and enhance adaptive thinking.

SCENARIO PLANNING

What it is: Scenario planning involves envisioning different possible futures and developing strategies for each scenario.

How it helps adaptive thinking: It helps individuals or teams think through multiple possible outcomes, preparing them to respond effectively to unexpected changes or challenges.

Use: Leaders and decision-makers use scenario planning to explore how different factors (e.g., market shifts and economic conditions) might affect outcomes and to devise strategies for various situations.

MIND MAPPING

What it is: Mind mapping is a visual tool for organizing information around a central idea. It helps break down complex problems into manageable components and identify relationships between them.

How it helps adaptive thinking: Mind maps encourage creative thinking by allowing you to visualize multiple ideas and solutions, helping you consider various alternatives to a problem.

Use: It is useful for brainstorming, problem-solving, or mapping out different potential responses to a situation.

SYSTEMS THINKING

What it is: Systems thinking focuses on understanding how different parts of a system interrelate and affect each other over time. It looks at problems in the context of the larger system.

How it helps adaptive thinking: It allows individuals to see how changes in one area might impact others, helping them adapt by anticipating consequences and adjusting their approach.

Use: It is especially useful in complex problem-solving situations, such as organizational change or environmental challenges.

THE "WHAT-IF" TECHNIQUE

What it is: The "What-If" technique involves imagining different hypothetical situations to explore possible outcomes and develop plans for various scenarios.

How it helps adaptive thinking: It encourages individuals to prepare for uncertainty by considering alternative scenarios and planning for potential changes.

Use: This technique is helpful in risk management, contingency planning, and strategic decision-making.

SWOT ANALYSIS (STRENGTHS, WEAKNESSES, OPPORTUNITIES, THREATS)

What it is: Cognitive reframing involves changing how you interpret a situation, often by viewing challenges or setbacks from a new perspective.

How it helps adaptive thinking: It encourages flexibility in thinking, helping individuals change negative or rigid thought patterns and leading to more constructive and adaptive responses to problems.

Use: This tool is often used in therapy but can be applied in personal development or leadership training to improve resilience and adaptive thinking.

5.4 TECHNIQUES FOR STAYING FLEXIBLE AND OPEN-MINDED

Staying flexible and open-minded in an adaptive world is essential for navigating change, solving problems, and seizing opportunities. We need to believe that abilities and intelligence can be developed through effort, learning, and persistence.

To do this, we must embrace a growth mindset and view challenges as opportunities to learn rather than obstacles. For this, replace "I cannot do this" with "There must be a way; I just need to find it." Also, seek feedback and use it to improve.

Active listening has rewards, and we need to practice it. It is about fully engaging with others' perspectives without judgment or interruption.

How to practice:

- Listen to understand, not just to respond.
- Ask open-ended questions to explore different viewpoints.
- Avoid dismissing ideas that seem unfamiliar or unconventional.

Physical and mental health can wear you down if you allow it to overwhelm you. In work or personal life, you need to maintain your physical and mental health to handle stress and adapt to change.

How to practice:

- Exercise regularly to boost energy and resilience.
- Practice mindfulness to stay focused and calm.
- Prioritize sleep and nutrition to maintain peak performance.

We must also approach situations with curiosity and openness as if we were a beginner.

How to practice:

- Let go of assumptions and preconceived notions.
- Be willing to unlearn old habits and relearn new ones.
- Stay humble and acknowledge that there is more to learn.

Taking time to evaluate your experience and extract lessons is essential to remaining agile and continuously adaptive to situations around you.

How to practice:

- Keep a journal on your successes and areas you need to improve.
- Conduct regular "after-action reviews" for projects or decisions.
- Use insights from reflection to improve future actions.

By incorporating these techniques into your daily life, you can build the flexibility and open-mindedness needed to thrive in an ever-changing world. The key is to remain proactive, curious, and resilient in the face of uncertainty.

5.5 KEY TAKEAWAY

To **effectively adopt adaptive thinking** in our daily work life, we need to embrace flexibility, creativity, and a willingness to learn and adjust as situations change. Start by staying open to new ideas and perspectives, even if they challenge your usual way of doing things. For example, if a colleague suggests a different approach to a project, consider it with an open mind rather than dismissing it outright.

Next, practice **problem-solving with adaptability** in mind. When faced with a challenge, brainstorm multiple solutions and be willing to experiment. If one approach does not work, pivot quickly and try another. For instance, if a marketing campaign is not delivering results, analyze the data, gather feedback, and adjust the strategy accordingly.

Use **critical thinking** to assess situations objectively. Gather relevant information, identify patterns, and evaluate options before making decisions. However, balance this with **adaptive thinking** by remaining flexible and ready to change course if new information or circumstances arise. For example, if a project timeline is disrupted, reassess priorities and reallocate resources to stay on track.

Stay curious and committed to **continuous learning**. Seek out new skills, knowledge, and experiences that can help you adapt to changing demands. For instance, take online courses, attend workshops, or learn from colleagues to stay ahead in your field.

Communicate adaptively by tailoring your approach to the needs of your audience and the situation. In a team meeting, for example, you might switch between providing clear instructions, encouraging collaboration, or offering support depending on what the team needs at that moment.

Finally, build **resilience** by viewing setbacks as opportunities to learn and grow. When things do not go as planned, reflect on what went wrong, extract lessons, and apply them to future efforts. For example, if a presentation does not go well, analyze the feedback, improve your skills, and approach the next one with confidence.

By combining **critical thinking** (to analyze and evaluate) with **adaptive thinking** (to adjust and innovate), you can effectively adopt adaptive thinking in your daily work life. This approach ensures you remain flexible, creative, and resilient, enabling you to navigate challenges, seize opportunities, and thrive in a constantly changing environment.

PART 3

SITUATIONAL LEADERSHIP: LEADING WITH FLEXIBILITY

"Effective leaders must be flexible and adapt themselves according to the situation."

– Paul Hersey and Kenneth Blanchard

The world has changed a lot since the COVID-19 pandemic began. The crisis pushed organizations to quickly adapt to remote work, new technologies, and shifts in how customers behave. In this new reality, leadership styles have also evolved, with **situational leadership** becoming a key approach to help businesses navigate uncertainty and change.

Situational leadership is all about flexibility. It means leaders adjust their style to fit the needs of their team or the situation at hand. This approach is more important than ever in today's post-COVID world, where things are unpredictable and constantly changing. Leaders who can switch between giving clear directions, coaching, offering support, or stepping back to let their team take charge are better equipped to build resilience and encourage innovation.

Situational leadership is all about being able to lead effectively during tough times. It allows leaders to provide guidance when needed, offer support during challenges, and empower their team as things stabilize. By staying in tune with the needs of their organization and employees, leaders can handle crises with confidence and adaptability.

Five years after the pandemic started, the business world looks very different, and so does leadership. Situational leadership, with its focus on adaptability, empathy, and tailoring approaches to individual needs, has become a crucial tool for guiding organizations through uncertainty. As leaders face ongoing changes, embracing this approach is essential for fostering innovation, inclusion, and resilience.

Chapter 6

SITUATIONAL LEADERSHIP

6.1 WHAT IS SITUATIONAL LEADERSHIP

Situational Leadership is a leadership theory developed by Paul Hersey and Ken Blanchard in the late 1960s. It is based on the idea that no single leadership style is best for all situations. Instead, effective leaders must be able to adapt their leadership style to the maturity, skills, and experience of the individuals or teams they are leading, as well as the specific demands of the situation at hand. The core concept of situational leadership is flexibility — leaders must assess the needs of their followers and adjust their approach accordingly. Leadership should be **dynamic** and **adaptive**, meaning that leaders should adjust their style based on the **maturity** or **readiness** of their followers, as well as the demands of the situation.

Situational leadership is an adaptive leadership approach where leaders are encouraged to modify their management style to suit the current work environment or the specific needs of a team or group. This style emphasizes the leader's ability to adapt to the organization's or team's demands, which helps enhance their effectiveness and drive greater success.

Situational leadership is flexible. It adapts to the existing work environment and the organization's needs. It is not based on a leader's specific skill; instead, the leader modifies the management style to suit the organization's requirements.

One key to situational leadership is adaptability. Leaders must be able to move from one leadership style to another to meet the changing needs of an organization and its employees. They must also have the insight to understand when to change their management style and what leadership strategy fits each new paradigm.

6.2 STYLES OF LEADERSHIP

According to Hersey and Blanchard, there are four main styles of leadership, and depending on the scenario, situational leaders may utilize one of these behavioral styles.

6.2.1 S1 TELLING (DIRECTING)

- **Leadership Behavior**: In the **Telling** style, the leader provides **clear instructions** and specific guidance. The leader is highly directive but provides **low support**. The focus is on getting the task done. This style is featured by one-way communication. Generally, the team or the individuals do not have enough skill/knowledge at this level. Hence, they require detailed directions. The leader defines the role of subordinates by providing them with how, what, where, when, and why to accomplish a task. This style is a top-down approach where the employees just follow the directions of their leader.

- **Follower Characteristics**: This style is most effective when followers are **new, inexperienced**, or lack the necessary skills and knowledge to perform a task. They need **high direction** and **minimal support**.

- **When to Use**: This style is ideal for **M1 (Low readiness)** followers who need clear, step-by-step directions.

6.2.2 S2 SELLING (COACHING)

- **Leadership Behavior**: The **Selling** style is more **collaborative** and **supportive**. The leader provides a high level of direction, but also offers **high support**, focusing on motivation and development. The leader engages in a more two-way communication process that provides socio-emotional support while the leader is still furnishing the individual or team with directions that influence them to get on track. Even though the leadership style is moderately autocratic, it still requires some direction from the leader; nevertheless, some input from the employees are considered before implementing the decision.

- **Follower Characteristics**: This style is best when followers are **willing** but may lack the **skills or experience** required. They may need **encouragement** and **motivation** to become more confident in their abilities.

- **When to Use**: This style is most effective for **M2 (Moderate readiness)** followers who have some ability but lack full competence and need development.

6.2.3 S3 PARTICIPATING (SUPPORTING)

- **Leadership Behavior**: In the **Participating** style, the leader provides **low direction** and **high support**. The leader focuses on encouraging and empowering followers. Decision-making is more **shared**, and the leader acts as a facilitator rather than a director. At this level of development, participative decision-making exists regarding the accomplishment of tasks, while the leader exhibits low task behavior and maintains a high relationship behavior. This style mostly reflects democratic behavior, which passes more responsibility onto the employees. The leader authorizes the individual or the team to create their goals while he works along with them. The focus here is to develop the individual or team further to act and think autonomously, slowly releasing the leash and fabricating scope for self-leadership.

- **Follower Characteristics**: This style works when followers have the skills and capabilities to complete the task but may lack **confidence** or **motivation** to take full ownership of their work. They are generally competent but need support and encouragement.

- **When to Use**: This style is most effective for **M3 (High readiness)** followers who can perform tasks but need emotional support, guidance, or reassurance.

6.2.4 S4 DELEGATING

- **Leadership Behavior**: The **Delegating** style involves **low direction** and **low support**. The leader gives the follower full responsibility for decision-making and problem-solving, offering little guidance or supervision. The leader believes that the individual or team is now competent. This is a hands-off approach with the teams exhibiting high development levels. In this phase, the involvement of the leader with his employees is very minimal, and the goal-creation and decision-making responsibilities are delegated to the group or the individual. The leader is generally kept abreast through regular updates and is mainly involved in monitoring progress.

- **Follower Characteristics**: This style is used when followers are **highly competent, self-sufficient**, and **motivated**. They have the skills, experience, and confidence to perform tasks without much input from the leader.

- **When to Use**: This style is appropriate for **M4 (very high readiness) followers who are highly skilled and independent** and can complete the task with little or no assistance from the leader.

6.3 STAGES OF EMPLOYEE DEVELOPMENT IN SITUATIONAL LEADERSHIP

Along with leadership qualities, Hersey and Blanchard defined four types of development levels for employees.

6.3.1 D1 (Low Competence; High Commitment)

- Generally lacking the specific skills required for the job and lacks any confidence and/or motivation to tackle it.

6.3.2 D2 (Low-Some Competence; Low Commitment)

- May have some relevant skills but will not be able to do the job without help. The task or the situation may be new to them.

6.3.3 D3 (Moderate-High Competence; Variable Commitment)

- Experienced and capable but may lack the confidence to do it alone or the motivation to do it well / quickly.

6.3.4 D4 (High Competence; High Commitment)

- Experienced at the job, and comfortable with their own ability to do it well. May even be more skilled than the leader.

Development levels are situational and can change depending on the task at hand. A person may generally be skilled, confident, and motivated in their role but still find themselves at **Development Level D1** when faced with a task that requires unfamiliar skills. For example, many managers operate at **D4** when managing their department's daily operations but may drop to **D1 or D2** when handling a sensitive employee issue.

According to Blanchard and Hersey's leadership model, a leader's **Leadership Style (S1 - S4)** should align with the **Development Level (D1 - D4)** of their followers, meaning the leader must adapt.

For instance, if a new employee joins the team and is expected to process orders on their first day without proper guidance, they are at **D1**. Still, the leader, by stepping away, has taken an **S4 (delegating) approach** — resulting in confusion and frustration for the new employee and uncompleted work.

Conversely, if an experienced colleague is taking over responsibilities before a leader goes on holiday and is given detailed instructions for every task, they are at **D4**, but the leader has taken an **S1 (directing) approach**, which is unnecessary and ineffective. Matching the right leadership style to the follower's development level is crucial for success.

The work may still get done, but not as expected, and your experienced colleague may feel frustrated or resentful for being treated as if they lack competence. However, if the situations are reversed, the outcomes improve. Providing a new team member with detailed instructions and a checklist will help them feel supported and capable, while a quick conversation and a few notes will be sufficient for an experienced colleague before you go on holiday.

By aligning leadership style with the follower's development level, tasks are completed effectively; relationships are strengthened, and — most importantly — the follower continues to grow, eventually reaching **D4**, benefiting both them and the organization.

6.4 FOLLOWER READINESS/DEVELOPMENT LEVELS

Follower readiness (also called development) refers to the **ability** and **willingness** of followers to perform a specific task or role. The Situational Leadership Model categorizes follower readiness into four levels:

6.4.1 M1 (LOW READINESS)

- **Characteristics**: Followers in this group are neither able nor willing to perform a task effectively. They may lack experience, competence, or motivation.

- **Leadership Need**: They require **clear direction and close supervision** to accomplish tasks.

6.4.2 M2 (MODERATE READINESS)

- **Characteristics**: Followers are willing to take on tasks but lack the necessary skills or knowledge to perform them competently. They may need guidance, training, and development.

- **Leadership Need**: They need a **coaching** style with high direction and high support to build their skills and motivation.

6.4.3 M3 (HIGH READINESS)

- **Characteristics**: Followers are competent and capable but may lack confidence, motivation, or initiative. They may be able to perform tasks well but need emotional support and encouragement.

- **Leadership Need**: A **supporting** leadership style that provides **low direction,** but **high support** is needed to keep them motivated and ensure they stay on track.

6.4.4 M4 (VERY HIGH READINESS)

- **Characteristics**: Followers in this group are highly competent, experienced, and confident. They can work independently and take full responsibility for their tasks.

- **Leadership Need**: A **delegating** leadership style, where the leader offers **low direction** and **low support**, is appropriate, as the followers can make decisions and manage tasks on their own.

6.5 THE PROCESS OF SITUATIONAL LEADERSHIP

The process of situational leadership involves the leader assessing the follower's readiness level and then adapting their leadership style accordingly. Here is how this process works in practice.

1. **Assess the Follower's Readiness**: The leader first evaluates the follower's ability and willingness to perform the task. Are they competent, experienced, and motivated?

2. **Choose the Appropriate Leadership Style**: Based on the follower's readiness level, the leader then chooses the appropriate leadership style. For example, if the follower is new and inexperienced (M1), the leader will use a **directing** style. If the follower is skilled but lacks confidence (M3), the leader will use a **supporting** style.

3. **Monitor and Adjust**: Situational leadership is dynamic, meaning that as the follower gains more skills, confidence, and experience, the leader adjusts their style accordingly. Over time, the leader should shift from directing to coaching, supporting, and eventually delegating as the follower's readiness increases.

4. **Maintain Flexibility**: Situational leadership requires constant assessment and flexibility. Leaders need to stay aware of the changing needs of their followers and adjust their leadership behavior as the situation evolves.

The benefits of situational leadership include flexibility, as leaders can adapt their style to suit different situations and the needs of their followers, making them more effective in various circumstances. It also fosters employee development, as adjusting leadership styles to match followers' readiness promotes growth and helps individuals reach their full potential. Additionally, situational leadership increases motivation by offering the right support and challenge, boosting follower engagement, confidence, and enthusiasm. Finally, by applying the most suitable leadership style for each situation, leaders can enhance team performance, ensuring tasks are completed efficiently and effectively.

Situational Leadership is a highly adaptable and flexible leadership model that suggests the most effective leadership style depends on the followers' readiness level and the task demands. It highlights the importance of leaders being responsive to the development levels of their followers and adjusting their leadership behaviors accordingly. By using the appropriate style — directing, coaching, supporting, or delegating — leaders can enhance team performance, foster employee growth, and improve overall organizational success. However, decisive judgment and continuous assessment are required to be effective. Leaders must be able to accurately assess the readiness of followers, which can be subjective. Misjudging readiness can lead to applying the wrong leadership style, creating confusion or hindering progress.

There also tends to be an over-reliance on the leader as situational leadership heavily emphasizes the leader's ability to adapt. The model may not work effectively if a leader lacks awareness, judgment, or adaptability.

Chapter 7

ASSESSING AND ADAPTING TO SITUATIONAL NEEDS

7.1 THE ROLE OF FLEXIBILITY AND ADAPTABILITY IN LEADERSHIP

Flexibility and adaptability are critical traits for effective leadership, especially in today's fast-paced, ever-changing world. Leaders who embody these qualities can navigate uncertainty, inspire their teams, and drive success even in challenging environments.

Leaders must guide their teams through unpredictable situations like market shifts, technological advancements, or global crises. To achieve this, flexible leaders can pivot strategies quickly to respond to new challenges, while adaptable leaders remain calm and composed, providing stability and direction during turbulent times.

It builds resilient teams as leaders can set the tone for how teams respond to setbacks and challenges. Leaders inspire their teams to embrace change and learn from failures by modeling adaptability. Flexible leaders create a culture of resilience where teams feel empowered to adapt and grow.

Adaptable leaders make better decisions by considering multiple perspectives and adjusting their approach as new information emerges. They avoid rigid thinking and are willing to revise their plans when necessary. They balance data-driven insights with intuition and creativity to make informed, dynamic decisions.

Leaders who are flexible and adaptable are more attuned to their team members' needs and concerns. They create a supportive environment where employees feel heard and valued. They adapt their leadership style to meet individuals' unique needs, fostering trust and loyalty.

Leaders must navigate the complexities of working with teams that have diverse backgrounds, perspectives, and working styles. Flexible leaders adapt communication and management styles to connect with and motivate diverse team members. They foster inclusivity by being open to different ideas and approaches.

In times of crisis, leaders must act decisively while remaining open to changing circumstances. Flexible leaders can quickly reassess situations and adjust plans to address emerging challenges. They maintain transparency and communicate effectively, keeping their teams informed and motivated.

Flexibility and adaptability enable leaders to respond effectively to change, inspire their teams, and drive organizational success. These traits are essential for fostering innovation, building resilience, and maintaining a competitive edge in a dynamic world. Leaders who prioritize adaptability create a culture of continuous learning, collaboration, and growth, positioning their organizations for long-term success.

By embracing flexibility and adaptability, leaders can navigate complexity, empower their teams, and achieve sustainable results in an ever-evolving world.

7.2 ASSESSING AND ALIGNING SITUATIONAL NEEDS

Assessing situational needs and matching them to team members' development levels is a critical skill for effective leadership. This process involves understanding both the demands of the situation and the capabilities of your team members. You can use this step-by-step guide to help you evaluate and align these factors.

STEP 1: UNDERSTAND THE SITUATION

Identify the Task or Goal: Clearly define what needs to be accomplished. Consider the complexity, urgency, and importance of the task.

Assess the Environment: Evaluate external factors such as market conditions, organizational culture, and available resources.

Determine the Skills Required: Break down the task into the specific skills, knowledge, and behaviors needed to succeed.

STEP 2: EVALUATE TEAM MEMBERS' DEVELOPMENT LEVELS

Use frameworks like the Situational Leadership Model (developed by Paul Hersey and Ken Blanchard) to assess team members' competence and commitment levels. The model identifies four development levels:

D1: LOW COMPETENCE, HIGH COMMITMENT

Team members are enthusiastic but lack the skills or experience to perform the task effectively.

Example: A new hire eager to learn but unfamiliar with the company's processes.

D2: LOW TO SOME COMPETENCE, LOW COMMITMENT

Team members have some skills but may lack confidence or motivation.

Example: An employee who has basic skills but feels overwhelmed by the complexity of the task.

D3: MODERATE TO HIGH COMPETENCE, VARIABLE COMMITMENT

Team members are skilled but may lack confidence or be hesitant to take full responsibility.

Example: A seasoned employee who can perform the task but doubts their ability to lead a project.

D4: HIGH COMPETENCE, HIGH COMMITMENT

The team members are highly skilled, confident, and motivated.

Example: A top performer who consistently delivers excellent results and takes initiative.

STEP 3: MATCH DEVELOPMENT LEVELS TO SITUATIONAL DEMANDS

Once you have assessed the situation and your team members' development levels, align them using the following leadership styles from the Situational Leadership Model:

S1: DIRECTING (HIGH DIRECTIVE, LOW SUPPORTIVE)

This style is best for **D1** team members as it provides clear instructions, close supervision, and frequent feedback.

Example: A manager guiding a new employee step-by-step through a task.

S2: COACHING (HIGH DIRECTIVE, HIGH SUPPORTIVE)

This style suites best for **D2** team members. This style offers guidance and support while encouraging participation and building confidence.

Example: A manager working closely with an employee to develop their skills and address challenges.

S3: SUPPORTING (LOW DIRECTIVE, HIGH SUPPORTIVE)

This style is most suitable for **D3** team members as it focuses on collaboration, listening, and facilitating decision-making.

Example: A manager empowering a skilled but hesitant employee to take ownership of a project.

S4: DELEGATING (LOW DIRECTIVE, LOW SUPPORTIVE)

The group most suited for this style is **D4** team members as it provides autonomy and trust, allowing them to take full responsibility.

Example: A manager assigning a complex project to a top performer with minimal oversight.

STEP 4: USE TOOLS AND TECHNIQUES FOR ASSESSMENT

Performance Reviews: Regularly evaluate team members' skills, achievements, and areas for improvement.

360-Degree Feedback: Gather input from peers, subordinates, and supervisors to get a holistic view of a team member's capabilities.

Skill Assessments: Use tests, simulations, or practical exercises to measure specific competencies.

One-on-One Meetings: Have open conversations to understand team members' confidence levels, motivations, and concerns.

STEP 5: ADJUST YOUR APPROACH AS NEEDED

You need to keep your eye on progress and regularly check how your team is doing and see if the situation has shifted. It is also to be present with their team and give helpful feedback by sharing constructive advice to help the team improve or adapt. You would also need to reevaluate growth. As your team members learn and become more confident, there is a need for you to change your leadership style to match their new level of skill and readiness.

Here is an example of a scenario to help with your learning.

SITUATION: Your team needs to launch a new product within a tight deadline.

The task requires technical expertise, project management skills, and creativity.

Team member A (D1): New to the team, eager but lacks experience.

Team member B (D3): Skilled but hesitant to lead.

Team member C (D4): Highly competent and confident.

ACTION:

Team member A (D1): Provide clear instructions and close supervision (S1: Directing)

Team member B (D3): Offer support and encouragement while allowing them to take the lead. (S3: Supporting)

Team member C (D4): Delegate responsibility and trust them to manage their part of the project. (S4: Delegating)

By systematically assessing situational needs and team members' development levels, you can tailor your leadership approach to maximize performance, foster growth, and achieve organizational goals. This adaptive approach ensures that both the situation and the individuals are set up for success.

7.3 ENHANCING SITUATIONAL LEADERSHIP WITH CRITICAL AND ADPATIVE THINKING

Critical thinking and **adaptive thinking** are two essential cognitive skills that enhance **situational leadership** by allowing leaders to assess situations effectively, make informed decisions, and adjust their leadership style based on the needs of their followers and the dynamics of the environment. Both **critical thinking** and **adaptive thinking** are vital for effective situational leadership. Critical thinking enables leaders to assess their followers' needs, understand the situation, and make informed decisions. Adaptive thinking allows them to respond flexibly, adjusting their leadership style to meet changing circumstances. By integrating these two forms of thinking, leaders can enhance their ability to lead effectively, inspire growth, and navigate challenges, leading to better outcomes for their teams and organizations.

Critical thinking involves the ability to analyze information, assess situations, challenge assumptions, and make reasoned decisions based on logic and evidence. This type of thinking is crucial for leaders to identify the best leadership style in any given situation. Critical thinking can enhance situational thinking as it enables leaders to assess the skills, readiness, and potential challenges that followers face. This helps determine the appropriate leadership style (directing, coaching, supporting, or delegating) that matches the development level of their team members. They can evaluate various options and viewpoints. In situational leadership, this helps the leader choose the most effective response to a situation, balancing the needs of both the task and the people involved. Critical thinking helps leaders solve problems more efficiently. By breaking down a situation into its components and identifying underlying causes, leaders can adapt their approach to fit the specific context.

EXAMPLE: Imagine a project manager overseeing a team that is tasked with launching a new product. One team member is highly skilled but lacks motivation, while another is new and needs guidance but is eager to learn.

Using Critical Thinking: *The project manager critically assesses the readiness levels of both team members. For the highly skilled but unmotivated individual, the manager decides to use a **coaching** style (high support, high direction) to boost motivation. For the new team member, the manager uses a **directing** style (high direction, low support) to give clear instructions and guidance.*

Outcome: *Critical thinking allows the manager to adjust their leadership style based on an accurate evaluation of each team member's needs, resulting in better performance and development for both individuals.*

Adaptive thinking is the ability to respond flexibly to changes, uncertainty, and new challenges. It involves adjusting one's approach to meet the evolving demands of a situation, team, or task. In the context of situational leadership, adaptive thinking is key to recognizing when to change leadership styles and how to apply the most effective approach in response to the environment or followers' development.

Adaptive thinking helps leaders remain flexible when situations change unexpectedly. Whether it is a change in team dynamics, an unforeseen challenge, or a shift in organizational priorities, adaptive leaders can quickly adjust their leadership style to meet new demands. Situational leadership requires leaders to modify their approach based on the development level of their followers. Adaptive thinking ensures that leaders can tailor their style not only to the individual but also to external factors like team morale, workload, and organizational changes. Adaptive thinking encourages leaders to remain open to feedback and continuously improve their leadership approach. This promotes a growth mindset within the team, helping followers grow and evolve with the situation.

EXAMPLE: Consider a sports team leader (coach) managing a group of athletes with varying levels of experience and performance under pressure. The team has an important match coming up, but one of the key players sustains a minor injury.

Using Adaptive Thinking*: The coach quickly adapts their leadership style. For the injured player, the coach shifts to a* **supportive** *style (low direction, high support), offering encouragement and help with rehabilitation. For the rest of the team, the coach may shift* *to a **delegating** style (low direction, low support) because they are experienced and capable of adjusting their strategy independently.*

Outcome: *By adapting to the situation — managing the injured player's recovery while also empowering experienced players — the coach maximizes the team's performance and morale in a time of uncertainty.*

7.4 KEY TAKEAWAY

To **effectively adopt situational thinking** in our daily work life, we need to be flexible, observant, and responsive to the unique demands of each situation. Start by assessing the context — consider factors like the task at hand, the people involved, and the overall environment. For example, if you are leading a team, evaluate whether the situation requires clear direction, collaborative brainstorming, or hands-off delegation.

Next, adapt your approach based on the needs of the situation. If a team member is new and unsure, provide clear guidance and support. If they are experienced and confident, step back and empower them to take the lead. This flexibility ensures that your actions are aligned with what the moment requires.

Use **critical thinking** to analyze the situation objectively. Gather information, identify key challenges, and evaluate potential solutions. For instance, if a project is falling behind, analyze the root causes — such as unclear goals or resource shortages — before deciding on the best course of action.

At the same time, apply **adaptive thinking** to remain open to change and new ideas. If the situation shifts — like a sudden change in priorities or an unexpected obstacle — be ready to pivot your strategy. For example, if a client changes their requirements mid-project, adapt your plan quickly while keeping the team informed and motivated.

Communicate effectively by tailoring your message to the situation and the audience. In a crisis, be clear and decisive; in a brainstorming session, encourage creativity and open dialogue. This ensures that your communication is both appropriate and impactful.

Finally, reflect on the outcomes and learn from each experience. After addressing a situation, ask yourself what worked, what did not, and how you can improve next time. This continuous learning mindset helps you refine your situational thinking skills over time.

By combining **critical thinking** (to analyze and evaluate) with **adaptive thinking** (to adjust and innovate), you can effectively adopt situational thinking in your daily work life. This approach ensures that you respond to each situation with the right balance of structure and flexibility, leading to better decisions, stronger relationships, and improved outcomes.

PART 4

INTEGRATING CRITICAL, ADAPTIVE, AND SITUATIONAL THINKING

"The elements of leadership are responsibility, situational awareness, and initiative."

– Kathy Sullivan

In the post-pandemic context, integrating **critical thinking**, **adaptive thinking**, and **situational thinking** into leadership is crucial for navigating the rapidly changing business landscape. **Critical thinking** helps leaders make data-driven decisions by evaluating new market trends and understanding emerging challenges. **Adaptive thinking** enables leaders to quickly pivot and adjust strategies in response to unexpected disruptions or shifts in consumer behavior. **Situational thinking** allows leaders to customize their approach based on the unique needs of their team and the specific challenges they face, such as remote work or economic uncertainty. Together, these thinking styles enhance problem-solving, promote innovation, foster team resilience, and drive long-term success as organizations adapt to a post-pandemic world.

Chapter 8

THE SYNERGY OF CRITICAL, ADAPTIVE, AND SITUATIONAL THINKING IN LEADERSHIP

Integrating critical thinking, adaptive thinking, and situational thinking into leadership creates a cohesive, dynamic approach that enables leaders to navigate complexity, solve problems effectively, and lead their teams to success. Here are how these three thinking styles can be combined to form a robust leadership framework:

CRITICAL THINKING: THE FOUNDATION

Critical thinking involves analyzing information objectively, evaluating evidence, and making reasoned decisions. It provides the logical foundation for leadership decisions.

Role in Leadership:

It helps leaders assess situations, identify root causes of problems, and make informed decisions and encourages questioning assumptions and considering multiple perspectives.

How to Integrate:

ASK PROBING QUESTIONS: Use questions like "What evidence supports this?" or "What are the potential risks?" to challenge assumptions.

ANALYZE DATA: Use data and evidence to guide decisions rather than relying on intuition alone.

EVALUATE ALTERNATIVES: Consider multiple solutions and weigh their pros and cons before acting.

ADAPTIVE THINKING: THE FLEXIBILITY

Adaptive thinking is the ability to adjust strategies and approaches in response to changing circumstances. It ensures leaders remain agile and resilient.

Role in Leadership:

It enables leaders to pivot quickly when faced with unexpected challenges or opportunities and fosters innovation and creativity by encouraging experimentation and learning.

How to Integrate:

EMBRACE CHANGE: View change as an opportunity rather than a threat.

EXPERIMENT AND ITERATE: Test new ideas, learn from failures, and refine approaches.

STAY OPEN-MINDED: Be willing to consider unconventional solutions and adapt to new information.

SITUATIONAL THINKING: THE CONTEXT

Situational thinking involves assessing the specific context of a situation and tailoring actions to fit the unique demands of that moment. It ensures leadership is context-aware and responsive.

Role in Leadership:

Situational leadership helps leaders understand the nuances of a situation, including team dynamics, external factors, and individual needs. It allows leaders to adjust their style and approach to match the situation.

How to Integrate:

ASSESS THE ENVIRONMENT: Consider factors like team morale, organizational culture, and external pressures.

TAILOR YOUR APPROACH: Use frameworks like the Situational Leadership Model to match your leadership style to the development level of your team members.

BE CONTEXT-SENSITIVE: Recognize that what works in one situation may not work in another.

8.1 INTEGRATING THE THREE THINKING STYLES: A COHESIVE APPROACH

Below are the steps to combine all three thinking styles into a cohesive leadership approach.

STEP 1: ASSESS THE SITUATION (SITUATIONAL THINKING)

What to Do:

- Analyze the context, including the task, team dynamics, and external factors.
- Identify the specific demands of the situation and the skills required to address them.

  Example: If your team is facing a tight deadline for a high-stakes project, assess the urgency, complexity, and resources available.

STEP 2: ANALYZE & EVALUATE (CRITICAL THINKING)

What to Do:

- Gather and evaluate relevant information to understand the problem or opportunity.
- Identify potential solutions and weigh their pros and cons.

  Example: Evaluate whether your team has the necessary skills to meet the deadline or if additional resources are needed.

STEP 3: ADAPT & INNOVATE (ADAPRIVE THINKING)

What to Do:

- Be open to adjusting your approach based on new information or changing circumstances.
- Encourage creative problem-solving and experimentation.

  Example: If the team lacks certain skills, consider redistributing tasks, providing training, or bringing in external support.

STEP 4: TAILOR YOUR LEADERSHIP STYLE (SITUATIONAL THINKING)

What to Do:

- Match your leadership approach to the development level and needs of your team members.

- Provide the right balance of direction and support.

Example: For a team member who is new to the task (D1), provide clear instructions and close supervision. For a seasoned team member (D4), delegate responsibility and offer autonomy.

STEP 5: MONITOR & ADJUST (ADAPTIVE + CRITICAL THINKING)

What to Do:

- Continuously assess the effectiveness of your approach.

- Use feedback and data to refine your strategy and make necessary adjustments.

Example: If the team is struggling to meet the deadline, reassess the workload, provide additional support, or adjust timelines.

STEP 6: REFLECT & LEARN (CRITICAL + ADAPTIVE THINKING)

What to Do:

- After the situation is resolved, reflect on what worked and what did not.

- Use these insights to improve your leadership approach for future challenges.

Example: Conduct a post-project review to identify lessons learned and areas for improvement.

EXAMPLE SCENARIO: LEADING THROUGH A CRISIS

STEP 1: Assess the Situation (Situational Thinking)

A sudden market downturn has impacted your company's revenue. You need to cut costs without demoralizing your team.

STEP 2: Analyze & Evaluate (Critical Thinking)

You gather data on which areas of the business are most affected and identify cost-cutting measures that minimize layoffs.

STEP 3: Adapt & Innovate (Adaptive Thinking)

You begin to explore alternative solutions, such as reducing non-essential expenses, renegotiating contracts, or implementing remote work to save on office costs.

STEP 4: Tailor Your Leadership Style (Situational Thinking)

For anxious team members, provide reassurance and clear communication (S3: Supporting). For confident team members, involve them in brainstorming solutions (S4: Delegating).

STEP 5: Monitor & Adjust (Adaptive + Critical Thinking)

Track the impact of cost-cutting measures and adjust strategies as needed to ensure financial stability and team morale.

STEP 6: Reflect & Learn (Critical + Adaptive Thinking)

After the crisis, review the effectiveness of your actions and identify ways to build resilience for future challenges.

The key benefits of integrating these thinking styles include: (1) **Holistic Decision-Making**, which combines logic, creativity, and context-awareness to ensure well-rounded decisions. (2) **Agility and Resilience**, allowing leaders to respond effectively to change and uncertainty. (3) **Empowered Teams**, as it tailors' leadership to the individual and situational needs, fostering trust and engagement. (4) **Continuous Improvement**, which encourages reflection and learning, ultimately driving long-term growth and success.

By integrating critical, adaptive, and situational thinking, leaders can create a cohesive, flexible, and effective approach to leadership that thrives in today's complex and ever-changing world.

Chapter 9

LEADING TEAMS THROUGH CHANGE

Combining **analytical thinking** and **creative thinking** is essential for solving complex problems, especially in uncertain or dynamic environments, and it aligns perfectly with the principles of **critical thinking** and **adaptive thinking**. Critical thinking involves analyzing information, evaluating evidence, and making logical decisions, while adaptive thinking focuses on flexibility, creativity, and resilience in the face of change. Here is how these skills work together:

First, use **critical thinking** to break down the problem into smaller parts, gather relevant data, and identify patterns or root causes. For example, a company facing declining sales might analyze customer feedback and market trends to understand the issue. Next, shift to **adaptive thinking** by brainstorming creative solutions and exploring new perspectives. The same company might brainstorm ideas like revamping the product or launching a new marketing campaign.

Then, use **critical thinking** again to evaluate the feasibility of each idea, considering factors like cost, resources, and risks. The company might prioritize the most practical solutions, such as redesigning the product. After that, apply **adaptive thinking** to test and iterate on the chosen solutions. The company could prototype the redesigned product, gather feedback, and refine it based on the results.

Finally, use **adaptive thinking** to stay flexible and adjust strategies as the situation evolves. For instance, if the redesigned product does not perform as expected, the company might pivot to a new approach, like bundling products or offering discounts, while using **critical thinking** to monitor progress and analyze the impact of these changes.

In summary, combining **critical thinking** (analytical, logical, and evidence-based) with **adaptive thinking** (creative, flexible, and resilient) allows individuals and organizations to solve complex problems effectively. Critical thinking provides the structure and clarity needed to understand the problem, while adaptive thinking generates innovative and adaptable solutions. Together, these skills ensure that solutions are both practical and forward-thinking, enabling success in an ever-changing world.

9.1 CHANGETHROUGHADAPTIVECOMMUNICATION

To build trust and foster collaboration through **adaptive communication**, we can incorporate the principles of **critical thinking** and **adaptive thinking** in the following ways:

First, use **critical thinking** to actively listen and understand the perspectives, needs, and concerns of others. This means analyzing what is being said, asking clarifying questions, and avoiding assumptions. For example, in a team meeting, a leader might listen carefully to each member's input and summarize their points to ensure everyone feels heard and valued.

Next, apply **adaptive thinking** to tailor your communication style to the situation and the individuals involved. This could mean adjusting your tone, approach, or level of detail based on the audience's preferences or the context. For instance, when addressing a team during a crisis, a leader might use a supportive and empathetic tone to build trust, while in a brainstorming session, they might encourage open and creative dialogue to foster collaboration.

Then, we should use **critical thinking** to provide clear, logical, and evidence-based feedback. Constructive feedback helps team members grow and improves trust by showing that you are invested in their development. For example, instead of saying, "This is not working," a leader might say, "Here is what is working well, and here is how we can improve based on the data."

At the same time, we use **adaptive thinking** to remain flexible and open to feedback yourself. Show that you are willing to adapt your approach based on input from others, which builds trust and encourages a culture of mutual respect. For example, if a team member suggests a better way to approach a project, a leader might acknowledge the idea and adjust the plan accordingly.

Finally, we use **adaptive communication** to foster collaboration by creating an environment where everyone feels safe to share ideas and take risks. Encourage open dialogue, celebrate diverse perspectives, and emphasize teamwork over individual success. For instance, a leader might organize regular check-ins where team members can share updates, challenges, and ideas in a supportive setting.

By combining **critical thinking** (to analyze, clarify, and provide structured feedback) with **adaptive thinking** (to adjust communication styles and remain open to change), leaders can build trust, foster collaboration, and create a culture of transparency and innovation. This approach ensures that communication is not only effective but also adaptable to the needs of the team and the situation, strengthening relationships and driving collective success.

9.2 KEY TAKEAWAY

Integrating critical, adaptive, and situational thinking into personal and professional practices can yield numerous benefits.

	CRITICAL THINKING	**ADAPTIVE THINKING**	**SITUATIONAL THINKING**
ENHANCED PROBLEM SOLVING	Enables you to analyze problems systematically, identify root causes, and evaluate potential solutions.	Allows you to adjust your approach as new information or challenges arise, ensuring flexibility in problem-solving.	Helps you tailor your solutions to the specific context, increasing the likelihood of success.
IMPROVED DECISION-MAKING	Encourages you to weigh evidence, consider alternatives, and avoid biases, leading to more informed decisions.	Prepares you to pivot when circumstances change, ensuring decisions remain relevant and effective.	Ensures decisions are context-aware, considering the unique factors of each situation.

INCREASED RESILIENCE AND AGILTY	Builds mental resilience by fostering a mindset that questions assumptions and seeks evidence.	Enhances your ability to respond to unexpected changes, making you more agile in dynamic environments.	Helps you anticipate and prepare for different scenarios, reducing the impact of unforeseen events.
BETTER COMMUNICATION AND COLLABORATION	Promotes clear, logical communication by encouraging you to articulate your reasoning and evidence.	Facilitates collaboration by helping you understand and adapt to others' perspectives and working styles.	Improves your ability to communicate effectively in different contexts, ensuring your message is appropriate and impactful.
ENHANCED CREATIVITY AND INNOVATION	Challenges conventional wisdom and encourages exploration of new ideas.	Fosters a mindset open to experimentation and iteration, key components of innovation.	Encourages creative solutions tailored to specific contexts, leading to more practical and innovative outcomes.
GREATER STRATEGIC FORESIGHT	Helps you anticipate potential challenges and opportunities by analyzing trends and data.	Prepares you to adjust strategies in real-time as conditions evolve.	Ensures strategies are grounded in the realities of the current environment, making them more effective.

(Contd.)

IMPROVED RISK MANAGEMENT	Identifies potential risks by thoroughly evaluating all aspects of a situation.	Enables quick adjustments to mitigate risks as they emerge.	Assesses risks in the context of the specific situation, allowing for more precise risk management strategies.
PERSONAL AND PROFESSIONAL GROWTH	Encourages continuous learning and self-improvement by fostering a questioning mindset.	Builds confidence in your ability to handle change and uncertainty.	Enhances your ability to navigate complex environments, contributing to overall competence and growth.

Here are some practical steps for integrating all three critical thinking skills.

1. **Develop a Questioning Mindset:** *Regularly ask questions to challenge assumptions and explore different perspectives.*

2. **Stay Informed:** *Keep 'up-to-date' with relevant information and trends to make informed decisions.*

3. **Practice Flexibility:** *Regularly engage in activities that require adapting to new information or changing circumstances.*

4. **Reflect on Context:** *Always consider the specific context of a situation before making decisions or acting.*

5. **Seek Feedback:** *Use feedback to refine your thinking and adapt your approach.*

PART 5

BUILDING LIFELONG SKILLS

*"Tell me and I forget, teach me and I may remember,
involve me and I learn."*

– Benjamin Franklin

Chapter 10

DEVELOPING HABITS FOR CRITICAL, ADAPTIVE, AND SITUATIONAL THINKING

Sharpening thinking and leadership skills is not a one-time task but an ongoing process that requires **consistent effort** and a **commitment to growth**. It means dedicating time and energy daily to improving your thinking, making decisions, and leading others. For example, you might set aside time to read, reflect, or practice new skills regularly. It also involves being open to feedback and willing to learn from successes and failures.

This commitment to growth means staying curious, asking questions, and seeking new ideas, even when things are going well. It is about challenging yourself to step out of your comfort zone, whether trying a new approach at work, learning from people with different perspectives, or experimenting with creative solutions to problems.

At the same time, it requires discipline and focus. You need to actively work on improving your critical thinking, adaptability, and emotional intelligence, which are all key to effective leadership. For instance, you might practice active listening to understand your team's needs better or use reflective journaling to analyze your decision-making process.

Ultimately, sharpening these skills is about embracing a **growth mindset** — believing that you can always improve and that effort leads to progress. By making this commitment to growth a daily habit, you will become a better thinker and leader and inspire those around you to do the same. This continuous effort ensures you stay relevant, resilient, and ready to tackle the challenges of an ever-changing world.

Here are some daily practices you can adopt to stay curious, open to new ideas, and continuously improve.

1. ASK QUESTIONS DAILY

- Cultivate curiosity by asking questions about how things work, why certain decisions are made, or what could be done differently.

- *Example: "What can I learn from this situation?" or "How can we approach this problem in a new way?"*

2. READ AND LEARN REGULARLY

- Dedicate daily time to reading articles, books, or research related to your field or areas of interest.

- Explore diverse topics outside your expertise to broaden your perspective.

- *Example: Spend 20 minutes reading industry news or listening to a podcast on leadership trends.*

3. SEEK FEEDBACK

- Regularly ask for feedback from colleagues, mentors, or team members to gain insights into your strengths and areas for improvement.

- *Example: After a meeting, ask, "How could I have facilitated that discussion more effectively?"*

4. REFLECT ON YOUR DAY

- Take a few minutes at the end of each day to reflect on what went well, what did not, and what you learned.

- *Example: Keep a journal to track your progress and identify your thinking and behavior patterns.*

5. EMBRACE DIVERSE PERSPECTIVES

- Actively seek out and listen to opinions and ideas that differ from your own.

- *Example: In team discussions, encourage quieter members to share their thoughts and consider their input seriously.*

6. PRACTICE ACTIVE LISTENING

- Focus fully on the speaker, avoid interrupting, and ask follow-up questions to deepen your understanding.

- *Example: In conversations, paraphrase what you have heard to ensure clarity and show that you value the other person's input.*

7. SET LEARNING GOALS

- Identify specific skills or knowledge areas you want to develop and create a plan to achieve them.

- *Example: Commit to learning a new software tool or improving your public speaking skills within a set timeframe.*

8. STAY INFORMED ABOUT TRENDS

- Keep up with your industry's emerging trends, technologies, and best practices.

- *Example: Subscribe to newsletters, follow thought leaders on social media, or attend webinars.*

9. CHALLENGE ASSUMPTIONS

- Regularly question your own beliefs and assumptions to avoid biases and stay open to new possibilities.

- *Example: Ask yourself, "Why do I believe this to be true?" or "What evidence supports this assumption?"*

10. LEAD BY EXAMPLE

- Demonstrate curiosity and a growth mindset in your actions and decisions to inspire your team.

- *Example: Share what you have learned recently or admit when you do not know something, showing that learning is a continuous process.*

By incorporating these daily practices into your routine, you can sharpen your thinking and leadership skills while staying curious and open to new ideas. These habits foster a growth mindset, encourage innovation, and build resilience, helping you navigate challenges and lead effectively in a constantly changing world.

Chapter 11

TEACHING CRITICAL, ADAPTIVE, AND SITUATIONAL THINKING

Fostering **the three thinking and leadership skills** — and teaching them to others — requires creating an environment that encourages thoughtful, flexible, and innovative thinking. Here are some practical ways to do it.

1. ENCOURAGE CURIOSITY AND QUESTIONING

- Creating a culture where asking questions is valued and encouraged. Teach others to challenge assumptions and explore different perspectives.

- *Example: In team meetings, ask open-ended questions like, "What if we approached this problem differently?" or "What assumptions are we making here?"*

2. PROMOTE CONTINUOUS LEARNING

- Provide opportunities for learning and development, such as workshops, training sessions, or access to resources like books and online courses.

- *Example: Encourage team members to attend industry conferences or share key takeaways from a recent webinar with the group.*

3. MODEL REFLECTIVE PRACTICES

- Lead by example by regularly reflecting on decisions, outcomes, and lessons learned. Share your reflections openly to demonstrate the value of self-assessment.

- *Example: After completing a project, hold a debrief session to discuss what worked, what did not, and how to improve next time.*

4. FOSTER COLLABORATION AND DIVERSE PERSPECTIVES

- Build teams with diverse backgrounds, skills, and viewpoints to encourage creative problem-solving and innovative thinking.

- *Example: Create cross-functional teams for projects to bring together different expertise and perspectives.*

5. PROVIDE SAFE SPACES FOR EXPERIMENTATION

- Encourage risk-taking and experimentation by creating an environment where failure is seen as a learning opportunity rather than a setback.

- *Example: Allow team members to test new ideas on a small scale and celebrate the lessons learned, even if the outcome is imperfect.*

6. TEACH STRUCTURED PROBLEM - SOLVING

- Introduce frameworks like SWOT analysis, the 5 Whys, or the Six Thinking Hats to help individuals approach problems systematically.

- *Example: Use the Six Thinking Hats method to explore problems from multiple angles in brainstorming sessions.*

7. EMPHASIZE ADAPTABILITY AND FLEXIBILITY

- Encourage individuals to stay open to change and adapt their approaches as new information or challenges arise.

- *Example: During a crisis, guide your team to pivot quickly by focusing on solutions rather than dwelling on the problem.*

8. DEVELOP EMOTIONAL INTELLIGENCE

- Teach the importance of empathy, self-awareness, and effective communication in thinking and decision-making.

- *Example: Train leaders to recognize and respond to their team members' emotional needs, fostering trust and collaboration.*

9. ENCOURAGE FEEDBACK AND ITERATION

- Create a feedback-rich environment where individuals can share insights, critique ideas constructively, and refine their thinking.

- *Example: After presenting a new idea, ask for feedback and encourage the team to refine it collaboratively.*

10. LEAD WITH A GROWTH MINDSET

- Demonstrate a commitment to growth by being open to learning, admitting mistakes, and showing resilience in facing challenges.

- *Example: Share your learning experiences and how they helped you grow as a leader.*

Fostering these three thinking and leadership skills — and teaching them to others — requires creating an environment that values curiosity, collaboration, and continuous learning. You can cultivate a culture of thoughtful and flexible thinking by encouraging questioning, providing opportunities for experimentation, and modeling reflective practices. This approach not only enhances individual and team performance but also prepares everyone to navigate complexity, adapt to change, and thrive in post-Covid-19 world.

Chapter 12

THE FUTURE OF
THINKING AND LEADERSHIP

In the age of **AI (artificial intelligence) and automation, critical**, **adaptive**, and **situational thinking** are more important than ever, as they equip individuals and organizations to navigate the rapid changes and complexities brought by technological advancements. These thinking skills help bridge the gap between human capabilities and machine efficiency, ensuring that we keep up with technological progress and use it responsibly and effectively.

Critical thinking allows us to analyze and evaluate AI systems' outputs, ensuring they are accurate, reliable, and aligned with ethical standards. For example, while AI can process vast amounts of data, it takes human critical thinking to interpret the results, identify potential biases, and make informed decisions that consider broader implications. Without critical thinking, we risk blindly trusting AI, which can lead to errors, ethical dilemmas, or missed opportunities.

Adaptive thinking enables us to stay flexible and open to change as automation transforms industries and job roles. It encourages individuals to embrace new technologies, learn new skills, and pivot when necessary. For instance, as automation takes over repetitive tasks, adaptive thinking helps workers transition into roles that require creativity, emotional intelligence, and complex problem-solving — areas where humans excel and machines fall short.

Situational thinking ensures that we apply the right approach for each unique context. It helps leaders and teams determine when to rely on AI, when to trust human judgment, and how to balance the two. For example, while AI might excel at data analysis, situational thinking reminds us that human empathy and understanding are irreplaceable in customer service or conflict resolution.

Together, these thinking skills create a powerful framework for thriving in the age of AI and automation. They allow us to **complement AI's strengths**, such as speed and efficiency, while addressing its limitations, such as a lack of creativity or ethical reasoning. They also help us **drive innovation**, using AI as a tool to solve complex problems and create new opportunities.

Moreover, these skills ensure we **use AI responsibly**, addressing ethical concerns like privacy, bias, and job displacement. By combining critical, adaptive, and situational thinking, we can harness the benefits of AI and automation while minimizing risks, ensuring that technological progress serves humanity's best interests.

In essence, these thinking skills are not just tools for survival in the age of AI — they are the foundation for thriving in a world where human ingenuity and adaptability remain irreplaceable. They empower individuals and organizations to stay ahead of the curve, embrace change, and create a future where technology enhances, rather than replaces, human potential.

Here is how each type of thinking contributes.

CRITICAL THINKING IN THE AGE OF AI AND AUTOMATION

- **Analyzing AI Outputs**: Critical thinking helps individuals evaluate AI-generated data or decisions' accuracy, reliability, and ethical implications. For example, a manager might assess whether an AI tool's recommendations align with the company's values and goals.

- **Identifying Biases**: AI systems can inherit biases from their training data. Critical thinking enables individuals to recognize and address these biases, ensuring fair and equitable outcomes.

- **Making Informed Decisions**: As AI handles routine tasks, humans must use critical thinking to interpret results, weigh alternatives, and make strategic decisions that AI cannot.

ADAPTIVE THINKING IN THE AGE OF AI AND AUTOMATION

- **Embracing Change**: Adaptive thinking allows individuals to stay flexible and open to new technologies, workflows, and roles created by AI and automation. For example, employees might learn to use new AI tools to enhance their productivity.

- **Reskilling and Upskilling**: As automation replaces certain jobs, adaptive thinking encourages individuals to acquire new skills and transition into emerging roles, such as AI ethics specialists or data analysts.

- **Innovating with AI**: Adaptive thinkers leverage AI to drive innovation, combining human creativity with machine efficiency to develop new products, services, or solutions.

SITUATIONAL THINKING IN THE AGE OF AI AND AUTOMATION

- **Tailoring AI Use**: Situational thinking helps leaders and teams determine when and how to use AI based on the specific context. For example, a company might use AI for data analysis but rely on human judgment for customer interactions, requiring empathy.

- **Managing Human-AI Collaboration**: Situational thinking ensures that humans and AI work together effectively. Leaders must assess the strengths and limitations of both and assign tasks accordingly.

- **Navigating Ethical Dilemmas**: As AI raises ethical questions — such as privacy concerns or job displacement — situational thinking helps leaders make context-sensitive decisions that balance innovation with responsibility.

Why do these skills matter?

- **Complementing AI**: While AI excels at processing data and performing repetitive tasks, it cannot think critically, adapt to new situations, or understand nuanced human contexts. These thinking skills ensure that humans remain indispensable in the age of automation.

- **Driving Innovation**: Critical, adaptive, and situational thinking enables individuals to harness AI as a tool for innovation rather than being overwhelmed by it.

- **Ensuring Ethical and Responsible AI Use**: These skills help individuals and organizations address the ethical, social, and economic challenges posed by AI, ensuring that technology is used responsibly and for the greater good.

In the age of AI and automation, **critical thinking** ensures we use technology wisely and ethically, **adaptive thinking** helps us stay flexible and innovative in a rapidly changing world, and **situational thinking** allows us to apply the right approach to each unique challenge. These skills empower individuals and organizations to thrive alongside AI, leveraging its strengths while addressing its limitations and ensuring a human-centered approach to technological progress.

12.1 PREPARING FOR CHALLENGES AND OPPORTUNITIES

Preparing for the challenges and opportunities of the future requires a proactive approach to developing and applying **critical**, **adaptive**, and **situational thinking** skills.

Investing in continuous learning means making a commitment to lifelong education and recognizing that staying updated on emerging trends, technologies, and best practices is essential for personal and professional growth. This ongoing effort involves actively seeking new knowledge through formal education, self-directed study, or professional development opportunities, ensuring that individuals remain equipped with the skills and insights needed to adapt to an ever-evolving world. By prioritizing continuous learning, individuals can anticipate and respond to changes in their industry, adopt new technologies that drive innovation, and stay ahead of competitors who may not be as proactive in updating their expertise. Moreover, a commitment to lifelong learning fosters a growth mindset, where individuals are motivated to continuously improve, solve complex problems, and develop new competencies that enhance their effectiveness in various roles. In today's fast-paced world, investing in continuous learning enhances personal capabilities and ensures that individuals can contribute meaningfully to their organizations, navigate uncertainty, and seize new opportunities for success.

Fostering a growth mindset involves developing a mental framework that views challenges as opportunities for learning and improvement, rather than obstacles to avoid. It encourages individuals to embrace setbacks and failures as valuable experiences that provide lessons for future success rather than seeing them as reflections of personal inadequacy. By cultivating this mindset, individuals become more resilient and motivated to tackle difficult tasks, understanding that effort, persistence, and learning from mistakes are key components of achieving mastery and reaching their goals. A growth mindset also encourages openness to change, where instead of resisting new ideas or unfamiliar situations, individuals view them as opportunities for development and innovation. This mindset drives personal growth and fosters a culture of continuous improvement, where individuals and teams are encouraged to take risks, adapt to evolving circumstances, and persist through challenges, ultimately leading to greater achievements and success over time.

Leveraging technology as a tool means using advancements like artificial intelligence (AI) and automation to complement and enhance human thinking and decision-making processes rather than replacing them entirely. AI and automation can handle repetitive tasks, process large datasets, and provide insights that help individuals make more informed, data-driven decisions. However, these technologies should be seen as aids that free up human capacity for higher-order thinking, creativity, and strategic planning. For example, AI can analyze trends and predict outcomes, allowing decision-makers to focus on interpreting these insights and making judgment calls that require emotional intelligence, ethics, and context — areas where humans excel. By combining the strengths of both technology and human expertise, organizations can increase efficiency, improve accuracy, and foster innovation. This approach allows individuals to focus on complex problem-solving, relationship-building, and strategic initiatives. At the same time, technology handles the more transactional or routine aspects of work, leading to a more productive and effective outcome. Ultimately, technology enhances human potential and allows for smarter, more impactful decision-making in today's fast-paced, tech-driven world.

In conclusion, "Think, Adapt, Lead: Critical Thinking and Adaptive Leadership In An Ever-Changing World" highlights the pivotal role of **critical thinking**, **adaptive thinking**, and **situational thinking** in effectively navigating the complexities and uncertainties of today's fast-paced environment. **Critical**

thinking enables individuals to analyze information, evaluate perspectives, and make informed decisions that drive success. **Adaptive thinking** allows leaders and teams to remain flexible, quickly adjust strategies, and learn from challenges, ensuring they can respond to changing circumstances with resilience and innovation. Meanwhile, **situational thinking** empowers individuals to tailor their leadership style and decision-making approach based on each situation's unique context and needs, fostering a more effective and collaborative environment. Together, these three thinking approaches create a cohesive strategy for responding to the evolving demands of the world, ensuring individuals and organizations remain agile, solution-oriented, and capable of thriving in an ever-changing landscape.